An Indenture tripartite; by which ... Harvey; Robert Walden; and then ... the first day of July; and the le... and paye; or cause to be delivere... of the fellowship of Cappers in Coventry; All the yssues rente revennes and proffitte of the said Mesuage and garden; shall remayne (over all reparatons; and necessary charges) to bee payd and distributed as followeth; that is to saye; yearly to some poore men; householders in the Citty; and of the fellowship of Cappers as by the said Masters shalbe thought to have most neede; twelve pence in money; And that the fellowship or twelve of them at the leaste; shall yearly for ever; betweene the first of July and the last of August come into St: Michaells Church in Coventry; and praise God for the benefitte bestowed on them by the said Thomas Oken; and that they which so doe shall have of their Godly meeting; two shillinge of the said Rent to make the same recreation or refreshing; and the residue of the said rent to be ymployed to the maynteuance of the fellowship; And the ffeoffees covenant with the Bailiffe and Commalty of the town of Warwicke; that when there shall remayne but three of them alive; they shall enfeoffe ten others of the fellowship of Cappers of the said Mesuage and garden; to the same intente and purpose that the ffeoffment when itt shalbe renewed; shalbe by Indenture tripartite; under the seale of the Bailiffe and Comialty of War and the hande and seales of the old and new ffeoffees; and lease to be made but by wrytinge Indented; the one part the to bee under the seales of the ffeoffees and the other seale of the Bailiffe and Commalty of the towne of Warwicke).

Thomas Nynall; William Ashburne and Robert Penninton; sinc ffeoffees; by Indenture tripartite enfeoffe John Roe; William N... Ffrauncis Nynning; Christopher Owen; Hugh Harvey; Symo... Nynmyng; Nicholas Chambers; Thomas Atkin William Ashburne yonnger; and John Ashburne Cappers; of the same Mesuage and garden; then in the tenure of Thomas Waddesworth; in ... streete sometymes called Gosford streete; and then called Gosford warde; neere Jordan well; them; and their heires in fee An Indenture tripartite; annexed; of the same date; declaringe the same use as ...

John Roe; William Nynall; and Ffrauncis Nynmyng; the survivinge ffeoffees; by Indenture tripartite enfeoffe; Samuel Bonnor ... Owen; Henry Owen; Roger Millington; George Roe; Robert Sma... Potmow; Thomas Okersley; Roger ffisher; and ... ... Cappers; of the same Mesuage and ... Indenture tripartite annexed; of the same ...

The Mystery of
The Coventry Cappers

PETER KING

THE MYSTERY OF
THE COVENTRY CAPPERS

CONTINUUM
LONDON AND NEW YORK

CONTINUUM

The Tower Building

11 York Road

London SE1 7NX

370 Lexington Avenue

New York

NY 10017–6503

Continuum 2001

Copy editing: Katherine Lambert

Index: Angie Hipkin

Design: Bernard Madden

Cover photography: Manvir Rai – DLC

Hat line illustrations: John Hill

Typography and production: Lisa Davis, Steve Douglas and David Cadwallader

Cogent, Meriden, England

British Library Cataloguing-in-Publication Data

A catalogue record for this book is available from the British Library.

ISBN: 0-8264-5457-7

Printed and bound in Great Britain by The Bath Press

Bath, England.

Previous page: The entrance to the present Cappers' Room in 'old' Coventry Cathedral.

THIS BOOK IS DEDICATED TO
THE LATE LORD ILIFFE
(1918-1996)

Contents

AUTHOR'S NOTE

The Company and Fellowship of Cappers and Feltmakers which is alive and active in Coventry today descends from one of the many 'merchant' or 'craft' gilds which flourished in the Middle Ages over much of Europe and were an important part of the economic and political structure of its various nation states.

Sometime around World War I its members began to take a closer interest in their origins, and in 1921 a small booklet was commissioned from Miss Dormer Harris, a historian of medieval life. With the coming of the millennium in 2000 AD, the Cappers (as they now called themselves) decided that the time had come to produce a fuller story of their background.

Historians prefer to turn to original sources for their material, and in this respect the Cappers are fortunate in having preserved two old volumes. One is an Accounts Book for the years 1495 to 1925 and the other the Cappers' Order Book for the years 1639 to 1770 with a gap of about 30 years from the early Civil War period.

I am not a professional historian, but I wanted to have these two volumes transcribed (they are handwritten in difficult calligraphy in parts) because of their interest not only to the Cappers but to those interested to learn about life in medieval times. Using this material as a basis, I offered to write a popular history of the Cappers company. To put the gild in its context I have taken information from established modern historians of the medieval period which explains the kind of world in which the Cappers lived in the early years of their formation. As this is a popular rather than an academic study, I have not cluttered up the early pages with notes of sources but have indicated in Appendix III the major historical works from which I have borrowed. As for a bibliography, I quote A.G. MacDonnell's book on Napoleon and his Marshals: 'I confine myself to the simple statement that every single detail of this book has been taken from one or other work of history, reference, reminiscence or biography.'

PETER KING
Oxfordshire
December 2000

INTRODUCTION

THE WORDS 'CAPPER' AND 'FELTMAKER' AND THE DESCRIPTION 'GILDS'

T
he first meaning for the word 'capper' given by the *Shorter Oxford English Dictionary* is a capmaker, though there are other meanings related to the verb 'to cap', including a person or thing that caps all others. The origin of the term is likely to be the Latin *cappa* (or cap) which is in turn a covering for the head. This might even be a hood, or a head-dress for women, ordinarily worn indoors. In the sense in which we use the word today, though, the dictionary describes it as a head-dress of cloth, or the like, for men or boys, distinguished from a hat by not having a brim. It has been applied from medieval times also to many official, professional and special head-dresses. In the latter sense, it is used in the Roman Catholic church to describe a cardinal's biretta.

Another Oxford dictionary, giving extended information, explains that a cap is usually made of some soft material, and while this remains the case today, there are exceptions, like the hard hat worn by equestrians, known as a riding cap. Money is collected in his headgear by the professional. Other sporting headgear is similarly named, such as a cricket cap; to excel in the sport, one is 'capped'. At the other end of the scale, the cap and bells are the insignia of the jester.

The cap has, indeed, entered the language in such phrases as to put on one's thinking cap, to ask if the cap fits, and to set one's cap at a member of the opposite sex.

The word is flexible though, sometimes being used to describe what elsewhere is called a hat, and vice-versa. In one of his famous self-portraits, Rembrandt describes himself as wearing a cap, though its floppy structure, probably made of velvet, would most likely be called a hat today. He may have felt that by wearing a cap he was giving himself a certain grandeur. Conversely, marchers photographed on the Jarrow Crusade in the 1930s wear their caps (not a hat in sight) as a badge of the working man, even though the occasion signified that they did not in fact have a job.

The final irony is that if one wishes to purchase a cap today, it is necessary to visit a hatter, if one can be found. If not, a cap can probably be bought at what used to be called an outfitters, also not easy to find nowadays, though on market days, in the surviving country towns, caps are sometimes available on market-stalls in all shapes and sizes and appropriate colours, usually a tartan or some other rustic hue.

When this story of the Coventry gild begins, its members belong to an industry making woollen caps. Later, as will be explained, the gild also embraced members of the city's felt hat industry, known as Feltmakers.

The Oxford dictionary describes felt as cloth or stuff made of wool, or of wool and fur, or hair fulled or wrought into a compact substance by rolling or pressing. By 1450 the term 'felt hat' was so common that it came to be used for a hat of any material, especially when feltmaking spread to several different locations across the nation.

Feltmaking for hats continued well into the 20th century, as described in a paper reprinted in part as Appendix I to this book. The writer is Miss P.M. Giles, the paper 'The felt-making industry *c.*1500-1850 with particular reference to Lancashire and Cheshire', and she notes the existence of the Hatters Company of London and the Feltmakers Company of London. This book, however, confines itself to the Coventry Gild of Cappers and Feltmakers.

The bodies called gilds in this book refer generally to the craft gilds of Coventry, of which the Cappers were one. A fuller or alternative usage is the 'company' or 'fellowship' of Cappers. The word Capper is given an initial capital to differentiate it from 'capper' meaning the trade, or persons employed in it who had the monopoly of making knitted caps.

The spelling 'guild' or 'Guild' is not used here, except in special cases or quotations.

The term 'livery company' is not used here as this is more generally applied to the London gilds from which they derived. A history of these London companies says that the name gild, guild or geld, primarily meaning a payment (from the Saxon *gildan* – to pay) was variously applied in old times. It signified a tax or tribute, and was so used in the Domesday Book. It could also refer to an enfranchised district, as in the case of the wards of London which were called gilds.

The librarian to the Corporation of London, writing in 1834, makes the following observations which might equally apply to the Cappers. The gilds hold, he says, a high rank in city history by reason of 'their wealth – the important trusts reposed in them – the noble charities they support, and their connection with the civic constitution... [and] the earliest share [they had] in laying the foundation of British commerce... [Also] their Records are, for the most part, of remote antiquity and afford pictures of the Government, Religion, Custom, Habits and Expenses of former times'.

The 1921 history of the Cappers by Miss Dormer Harris says that the Cappers turned their attention to feltmaking when this craft was introduced to the city by Edward Owen, mayor in 1636. The gild's full name thereafter became as follows (quoting from the Minute Book, post 1670):

'The Master, Warden, Ancients, and Assistants of the Company and Fellowship of Cappers and Feltmakers of Coventry'.

A final note – the word 'mystery' was used to indicate a trade or other secret from the early 1500s and for an occupation from about the same time. The correct name for gild dramas, a miracle-play, was frequently misplaced by the term 'mystery play'.

A self-portrait etching made by
Rembrandt van Rijn in the
1630s. Long a resident of the
Jewish quarter in Amsterdam,
he incorporated their dress and
headgear in his biblical paintings,
and would himself routinely have
worn a hat in his studio.

CHAPTER I

'THE SACRED STAPLE AND FOUNDATION OF OUR WEALTH'

T he early 15th-century oil painting by Stefan Lochner shows his version of the Last Judgment. Frightful devils crowd round the gates of Hell and pull a group of naked creatures into the deepest abyss, where they will suffer eternal torture. Who are they? You can tell their status by their hats – a king, a dame, a bishop, a cardinal and a pope.

Lochner was a citizen of Cologne, Germany, one of the leading cities of Europe. England had no city in the same league, but a hundred years earlier than this, its rulers had been equally critical of those who decked themselves out in extravagant headgear. Edward III in 1363 introduced sumptuary laws (i.e. laws to restrict the display of magnificence) aimed against 'the outrageous and excessive apparel of divers people'. Knights might choose whatever cloth they pleased, except for gold, which was reserved for those lords at the top of the tree, and whose ladies might wear pearls in the embroidery of their head-dress. The lower orders were restricted to five or six marks-worth of broadcloth and a plain hat, and men working at hand-trades and yeomen were limited to cloth worth 40 shillings. Those below the rank of yeomen were to wear no cloth except russet wool or blanket.

Previous page: In the famous medieval oil painting by Stefan Lochner the status of those condemned to the tortures of Hell is indicated by the hats they are wearing – ranging from the dame to the most prestigious, who happens to be a pope.

To keep up with the medieval Jones's, therefore, one had to maintain a certain style of dress which declared one's office to the world at large – and one had to be prepared to meet the heavy taxation which such splendour attracted. So while the laws of Edward III may have brought him income, they did not result in a general shabbiness of attire amongst the population at large, which struggled energetically to be rich enough to afford the trappings of office, in particular headgear.

Coventry, one of the centres of the hat business, had never had it so good as in the 150 years following these sumptuary laws. The satirist Stubbs, in his *Anatomie of Abuses* (1583), railed against the fashion which 'be so rare and strange, so in the stuff whereof their hats be divers also; for some are of silk, some of taffetis, some of sarcenet, some of wool; and, which is more curious, some of a certain kind of fine hair. These they call Beaver hats, of twenty, thirty or fourty shillings price, fetched from beyond the seas, whence a great sort of other varieties do come.' Coventry did not make beavers but it prospered well with other types of hat – so much so that the city shot up to third position in the league of provincial towns. 'This', says Charles Pythian-Adams, 'was the period of greatest building activity, the foundation and growth of guilds and crafts, the nationally-famous Corpus Christi plays and the pageants. Coventry became one of the most beautiful cities in the kingdom.'

Most of its economic, social and political power and prestige was concentrated in the upper class of merchants, particularly mercers and drapers. For example, of the 94 mayors of the city listed by name between 1420 and 1547, some 57 were known to be wool merchants, mercers or drapers. By the 15th century the cappers had joined this select band. Again, the secret of their success was wool.

England was one of the four nations to depend for its wealth upon wool in medieval times (the others were Flanders, Tuscany and Castile). From the earliest days, we can imagine English shepherds sending their wool across the Channel to Flanders, until, after William conquered England, the Flemish returned to teach the English how to use the material that would replace fur and hide. From that time on it became 'the sacred staple and foundation of our wealth'. However, it is not until about 1200 that there is any direct contemporary evidence of actual cloth-making in Coventry itself. The city was more of a wool-trading than a cloth-making town at that time.

Over the next hundred years, up to 1300, weaving became ever more significant. Out of a total Coventry population of some 3500 there were 40 families with the surname Webb or Weaver or similar. Those named Dyer formed the second largest group, and there are others including Comber, Fuller and Walker. Records indicate that the cloth being made was dyed ('*panna tincta*') a phrase used only to describe high-quality cloth of the kind made for export. While this was going on, dealing in raw wool, which had been the core

The satirist Stubbs and others railed against the finery worn by the up-and-coming classes, particularly this headgear so rare and strange.

trade of the city, was declining and by the end of the 13th century the importance of the wool barons and their families was fading.

The mechanics behind cloth-making's growing supremacy were slow to change. It remained a 'cottage industry', though by the 13th century the English shepherds and their business associates were using 'technical' aids – disentangling wool by 'carding' with a pair of wire-tooth brushes, the wool being worked from one hand to another (previously this job was done by a teasel, a sort of thistle). Carding was superseded by 'combing' with metal teeth mounted on horn, with a wooden handle which allowed the worker to cut easily through

the wool. Then the spinning wheel arrived from China, tried out for the first time in Germany in 1280. This doubled productivity, but the job remained an individual task (often women's work) as there were virtually no factories. This remained the case even after the weavers' horizontal loom was devised. Finally the 'fulling' mill was invented (fulling involved washing) with power-driven mallets driven by waterwheels. In Coventry fulling was always known as 'walking' and its craftsmen as 'walkers' because they had originally pounded the 'Fullers' Earth' with their feet.

This single-hand loom in Coventry's museum dates from the 17th century but had not changed much from medieval times. For many workers it replaced the spinning wheel.

The weaver's loom, which replaced the spinner's wheel, would be set up in the main room of the worker's cottage, to which he would bring wool clipped from his own sheep. The spinners – perhaps his wife, daughter, or related 'spinsters' – helped with hand-held cards for carding, using distaffs and spindles. The peasant worker needed water to remove the grease from the cloth, and when it was woven he would dye it in one of the tubs of prepared water on the floor beside him. He might go to one of the publicly maintained watermills to have it 'fulled' or 'teased' for a fixed payment.

The average family unit making some kind of woollen cloth might have about an acre of land with not only sheep, but a cow, chickens, or a horse if the peasant fetched wool from nearby shepherds. The horse would also be used for journeys to the fulling mill, where the carded wool would be sold to merchants.

This rural employment unit was not yet superseded by the growth of towns, but the growing specialisation of the manufacturing processes of wool and cloth was undoubtedly a factor in the eventual separation of town and country life.

England was, at first, rather backward in the urbanisation process (compared to other leading European nations, particularly the great city centres of Flanders or Italy). Most English towns housed fewer than 1500 inhabitants; today such a number could be fitted comfortably into one tower block. But in medieval times, life in the towns was not fundamentally different from that in the rural countryside. One reason for this was that 'industry', particularly the wool industry, as already described, relied largely on domestic production. This was the case even after specialisation became more common – some families undertaking spinning only, others buying several looms. Merchants might put up capital for this kind of early industrial organisation,but in the main it was the peasants themselves who financed it.

Gradually the process known as 'putting out' meant that the weaver became less a part-time farmer and more a skilled workman. Increasingly, weavers would have enough to employ them in their wool business and to keep them away from any agricultural work except at harvest time.

There did not exist, therefore, a vast English proletariat surging to the towns from the rural areas. Such influx of non-natives as there was came about largely to replace those city dwellers who fell victim to the Black Death or other plagues. In the short period 1348-9 the Black Death carried off a third or possibly half the population. Yet we must not think that the medieval town, though it was more insanitary than the village, was a crowded slum. Its houses stood pleasantly in gardens, orchards and paddocks, and the number living together in the average town was small.

The predominant drive behind a wave of 'new towns' which developed in the 13th century was commercial, since the population explosion encouraged local lords to promote markets on their estates. As in present times, grants were available as incentives for residents to settle in growing towns, and the medieval peers themselves qualified for royal 'market' grants. Between 1200 and 1350, several thousand such grants were issued by the Crown so that every self-respecting town could have its market.

London of course was a-typical, even then being 'the great wen', with some 18,000 residents at its late-13th-century peak, compared to Bristol and Norwich, each with about 10,000 at their maximum. Ranking below them came about 10 centres including Newcastle, York, Boston, Ipswich, Coventry, Salisbury and Exeter. A number of reasons have been advanced for the success of one centre and the failure of others, amongst them their rôles as centres of exchange where they could service trades producing rural goods like wool, or supply them with manufactured goods.

Supporting such activities in a town were not only the residents but a large number of living-in 'servants' who were in truth apprentices and assistants in the family businesses. In the 1520s as many as one in four of Coventry's recorded population was made up of such servants, probably mostly youths and children.

But there was as yet no sign of an industrial revolution; true, there were already symptoms of organised activity in the larger wool-manufacturing towns of the Cotswolds and the early metal-working units at Birmingham, even though no large factory workforces existed. The employees here were subject to controls devised by the merchants who ruled the towns. They operated their controls to some extent through the gilds. The latter offered their members the social virtues of association, while in their economic role they served the interests of urban government – with the merchants at the top of the tree guiding the labour force made up of respectively craftsmen, journeymen and apprentices. One historian has described the gilds as 'industrial police' enforcing the policies of the ruling élite.

From the 14th century onwards, large towns like Coventry saw the formation of these trade gilds or fellowships in which master craftsmen were compulsorily enrolled, and from which they could be expelled if they broke the rules laid down by their wealthier peers and city fathers. The leading gild members acted as willing agents of the borough authorities, seduced by the status of office. Discipline was effected through the Leet Courts.

The development of the craft of capping was an example of this, effected within its new gild structure, as it superseded in importance other longer-established trades in wool and cloth in the years up to 1500.

Of course, not every citizen operated within the gild system. Each town also had its system of 'petty officers' with specific duties – constables of the peace, ale tasters, scavengers, rubbish carters and so on, and these men would hardly enjoy gild membership status, which was jealously guarded.

The gilds mentioned above were primarily economic in function. There was in addition another form of social group – indiscriminately called 'gild' or 'fraternity' at the time – which was a voluntary association of those living or working in the town, or in the nearby rural areas. Members would meet on market days, and annually for a feast. Religion played its part and focused loyalties on church buildings and on services with their rituals. Hence the popularity of religious processions and mystery plays.

Before examining in detail the gilds and their connection with religion, it is useful to look at the organisation of those industries which underpinned their culture and economies – chiefly wool and cloth. By now the big capitalists of this business had reorganised their industry and had set up a network to supply bales of cloth in quantity to London and other ports, from where it was exported all over Europe.

Wool, the basis of England's medieval wealth, was initially founded on the family unit which might rear and shear its own sheep and spin its own wool ready for processing.

England had previously relied for its markets for wool largely on sales of the raw material to the Low Countries and Italy, whose more advanced economies led the world in processing. After this time, England became a manufacturing nation in its own right, with cloth replacing raw wool as the main element in its international trade. Inevitably this led to changes in the location of this industry, as different areas exploited new manufacturing techniques.

For the first time, central government now intervened. Edward III needed money to finance his French campaigns and in 1303 imposed an additional levy on those foreign (alien) cloth exporters who operated from England. These levies further promoted the development of cloth manufactured in England, since they created a tariff barrier raising the costs of the raw material imported by the foreign manufacturers, to whom, it seems, the English passed on most of the wool tax. Flanders, overrun by the King's campaigning armies, also suffered an associated decline in textile trade. Conversely, the Dutch cloth industry expanded at the expense of the Flemish. English exports of cloth thus continued to rise until the end of the century and went on rising until the 1470s. By the beginning of the next century, cloth had replaced wool as England's main export. The difference between wool-cloth and cloth is described later.

The exploitation by the English of manufacturing improvements was a major factor in their export success, particularly their exploitation of water power. Water-powered washing (fulling) mills were not new, but the English machines had advantages over the Flemish wind mills. Also driven by water was the 'gig-mill' used for teasing woven cloth by teasels secured to rollers, which raised the nap on the processed cloth. This was then cropped with shears to give

A medieval painting which illustrates the importance of the hat as the crowning glory of the costume for both sexes on a festival day such as this.

it a smoother finish. Although English cloth became increasingly famous, it was not always the manufacturing areas that gained most benefit: London for instance still dominated the export trade, which was increasingly in the hands of the Merchant Adventurers company, itself dominated by the London Mercers company or gild.

Specialisation made for success, and Coventry became well known for its basic or staple woad-dyed blue cloths. Raw materials came from as far afield as Southampton, which was a distribution centre for long-distance trade in commodities connected with the cloth industry, notably dye stuffs such as woad. In 1456 Coventry succeeded in negotiating freedom from tolls in Southampton, which organised the supply of woad, much of it along the riverways

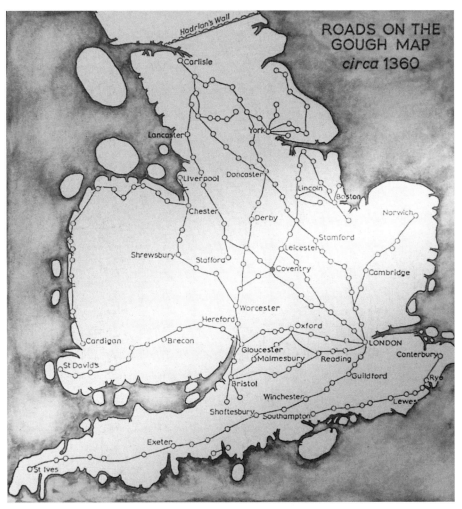

This version of the so-called Gough map originally drawn around 1360 shows Coventry's position as the great crossing point in the Midlands, perhaps the most important factor in its rise to fortune. It hangs today in the Herbert Museum in the city.

of the Itchen and the Test. So just as long-distance trucks bring components today from Southampton to the Midlands, so medieval shipping brought necessary wool-processing materials along the waterways.

Amongst other similarities between the present day and medieval times is the extent of state regulation. Innumerable Acts of Parliament laid down rules about the length, breadth, and weight of pieces of wool. Wool inspectors were appointed to ensure they were obeyed. Of course, the aim was to keep up the quality of English wool and cloth. And the rules were a success. One result was that the wealth of other states or city-states which used English wool also improved. Indeed the historian Hugh Thomas claims that the great barns of the Cotswolds helped to create the fortunes of the Medici and the Frescobaldi. Another historian says that Chaucer's fashionable contemporaries 'wore their estates upon their backs'.

Various statistics are used to illustrate England's mastery of the wool trade, but all give a similar picture. They show a shift in the distribution of national wealth in different areas of the country, with the north-east declining in favour of the south-east and south-west where they specialised in cloth. The shift from wool to cloth exports also had a dramatically favourable effect on many of the country's ports. London enjoyed the greatest growth of all. But Coventry's prosperity, though the city was nowhere near a port, was undoubtedly due to its location at a nodal point of inland communication. Skins and salt from Chester en route to London; wines from Bristol, fish from East Anglia, wood, alum and as noted, wool from Southampton. These were some of the goods which determined Coventry's growth, and which led to the formation of successful trades using those skills that were labour-intensive, the most significant being woven cloth, which took over from the export of wool itself.

CHAPTER II

'OF CLOTH MAKING SHE HADDED SUCH A HAUNT SHE PASSETH THEM OF YPRES AND OF GAUNT'

(CHAUCER'S WIFE OF BATH)

One of the major occupations of the medieval woman was operating her spinning wheel. Despite the fact that this was a man's world, women were thus a significant economic factor in that world. The women performed nearly all the preliminary processes such as combing and carding the wool. The craft of spinning, mainly practised by single women, led to the word 'spinster' being incorporated into the language as synonymous with an unmarried woman. As about five spinners were required to keep one male weaver going, the industry kept women employed far outside their own localities, and their woollen yarn was imported to all the major centres. Women were also engaged in weaving, but predominantly this was man's work.

The wife of the craftsman weaver, if she did not work as her husband's assistant in his trade, would eke out the family income by engaging in an occupation allied to his – for example spinning. Since not all women could marry, some spinsters practised a separate trade as a *femme seule*, unless, as many did, they joined a nunnery. Girls were often apprenticed to trades just as boys were, and so they went on to support themselves either as spinsters, or, if they were married, sometimes plying trades of their own quite distinct from their husbands.

It is true that some gild regulations expressly excluded women from

Chaucer's picaresque character, the Wife of Bath, was typical of the women who brought fame to English cloth, in the home market and also in Europe.

participating in trade, though exceptions were usually made for wives and daughters. Factories were, as previously explained, unknown, and craft work was carried on by the men in their own homes, so it was quite natural for their wives, as well as for journeymen and apprentices, to participate. In such cases, female apprentices were usually under the tuition of the master's wife. Textile manufacture was often organised on the 'putting-out' system – that is, merchants gave out raw material to workers in their own homes, thus facilitating further the employment of women.

Inevitably therefore, large numbers of widows carried on the trades in which their late husbands had specialised. Some gild regulations specifically allowed this, and the husbands, before they died, drew up wills providing for such activity to continue. Some widows even operated as merchants on a large scale in their own right, chartering ships like the merchants of Venice and having dealings with representatives of the King who levied taxes on his behalf for exports and imports. At the other end of the social scale, women worked as 'craftsmen' pure and simple.

In fact there was hardly a craft in which medieval women were not employed. They were butchers, chandlers, ironmongers, net-makers, shoe-makers, glovers, girdlers, haberdashers, purse-makers, skinners, bookbinders, gilders, painters, silk-weavers, embroiderers, spicers, smiths and goldsmiths and, of course, hat-makers. Excluding domestic or farm servants, the most numerous female occupations in one set of poll tax records were connected with the cloth trade. The biggest group were weavers, with a few dyers and some fullers. It was only natural that the widespread skills of these women craft workers should arouse jealousy in the male mind, and to assuage such prejudices the gild would keep non-relatives out – for example the Lincoln Fullers (wool-washers) ordered in 1297 that 'no one of craft shall work at wooden bar with a woman unless with wife of master or her handmaid'. The pretence was that such work as this was too hard for a woman, but in fact, most women would often do the same work as a man for a lower wage. Money was the dominant rationale, so women's wages were generally lower than the man's, even for the same work.

Women would also play their part in social or religious gilds, as they would – when permitted – in craft gilds. Yet in comparatively few crafts were women explicitly mentioned as members alongside male 'masters'; those who were deemed to be 'sisters' were usually widows. This was the case even in those crafts that were dominated by

It was natural for women to join their husbands in the processes of cloth-making, both in the home and, as in this illustration, in the garden.

In medieval times most of the English population, even those well-off, wore the same clothes as everyone else, and almost all of them wore hats, usually made of wool.

women – for example, silk weaving. The latter was regarded as the particular prerogative of better-class London citizens, and such 'silkwomen' took apprentices with indentures in the usual way. But the historian Eileen Power says 'women were rarely admitted as full members of the craft gilds, even in trades exclusively in the hands of women, such as the silk industry'.

It might be supposed that 'fashion' in cloth usage was largely down to the women workers. But historians suggest this is not the case. For example, everyone of either sex wished to have his clothes coloured if he could. The importance of colours in the symbolism of chivalry is well indicated in an epoch-making book, *The Waning of the Middle Ages,* by J.H. Huizinga. This historian pointed out that the symbolic meaning attached to blue and green was so marked and peculiar that it became almost impossible for people to consider wearing these colours except on special occasions. Hence the importance of dyeing, one of the most complex of early chemical processes, in which Coventry had a special place. 'Coventry blue' cloth came to be in demand all over the world. Hugh Thomas says that worldwide trade underlined the desire for fashionable clothes; he notes that the elaborate treatment of raw materials for those subservient to fashion is among the most deep-rooted of human attitudes, influencing profoundly agriculture, commerce, technology and methods of warfare. 'The manufacture of cloth [became] the chief industry by the age of agriculture, and, in the end, innovations in it indeed led to the transformation of the world.'

To return to medieval times, most of the English population, even the well-off, wore the same sort of clothes as everyone else. Women wore plain, loose-fitting garments and so did the men. The better-off might choose fine but simple linen, and this was as acceptable for a 'dress' occasion as a silk costume. However, by the 1530s and '40s, there was an explosive growth in the purchase of ornate (and costly) costume, led, naturally, by the wealthier citizens. Their dress became more formal as they aped Italian and Spanish fashions, and, after Elizabeth came to the throne, men's fashions changed entirely, becoming much more elaborate. One fashion historian decribes how 'aspiring courtier had to wear at least a quilted peacock doublet, a short cloak, trunk hose, starched ruffs, and an elaborate hat. Padded and ornately-designed breeches became the rage. Women [had] exquisitely decorated farthingales [a hooped skirt] and fine damask gowns.'

By the latter part of Elizabeth's reign, these extravagances of dress reached proportions never matched in England before or since. Historians call it a 'fashion madness' – rather as they did in the 1960s when Carnaby Street was at its height. What was fit for the upper classes was also aped by the lesser. Thomas Lodge, the literary gent, charged that ploughmen, previously content to wear wool, now desired fashionable doublets, and so farmers sold their sheep to pay for silk. Henry Traill, the Victorian writer, found evidence of Elizabethan gardeners wearing ruffs, hats trimmed with feathers, and full breeches called 'venetians'.

It is unlikely that those at the bottom of the social pile, the labouring peasants, spent much on such non-essential textiles. The living standards of the poor did not begin to improve until about 1650, and before that they actually fell and unemployment rose. The better-off, however, 'wore satin on solemn days, and chains of gold / a velvet hood, rich borders, and sometimes / a dainty miniver cap'. These were fashions that would change the lives of the Coventry Cappers and their friends.

CHAPTER III

'THE MOST NECESSARY
LUXURIES'

In the period up to 1500 England was still what we should now call an 'underdeveloped' country in relation to the major European nation states of the time – Italy, France, the Low Countries and southern Germany. There were only about four million inhabitants in England and Wales, while France had four times as many, Italy three times, and Spain nearly double. Economic historians describe England then as 'backward' and 'a country on the near-fringes of the European world'.

Most citizens of Coventry would have been unaware of their lowly status relative to Europe. Indeed, they were rather proud of themselves, as by the early 16th century their city was among the half dozen most important provincial towns in England. Before about 1570, the Cappers gild was one of the principal avenues of 'political mobility and a vital part of the community's social transformation' in the town. It continued, not surprisingly, to play a considerable role in the daily lives of Coventry's producers, shopkeepers and consumers 'long after its economic utility had passed'.

Until about 1550, most consumers relied upon markets for their everyday needs, and these markets met regularly in or near a town. Indeed, a town may have been defined by its possession of a market, just as we tend today to define a city as a community which possesses a cathedral. Gradually, towards the turn of the century, shops slowly

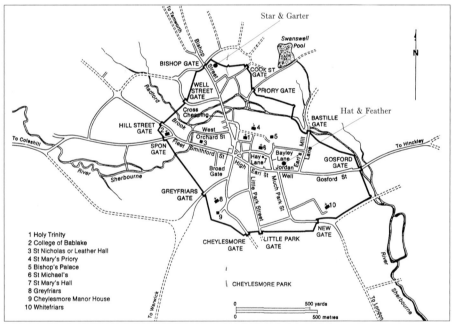

Above: a medieval representation
of Coventry.
Below: an adapted 15th-century
map showing the location of the
Capper-owned Hat & Feather and
Star & Garter.

replaced markets as the places where consumers purchased those goods they did not produce themselves. In addition there were fairs, which offered shops greater competition than did markets. The nobility, in particular, sent to fairs to buy commodities in large quantities to stock up their households. As for the middle classes, fairs did not compete directly with shops for their trade, though they did carry some of the same goods. Particularly after 1400, many fairs specialised in the sale of agricultural by-products such as cloth and yarn. However, shops gradually supplanted fairs as the principal source of luxury goods, and by the early 17th century the middle and upper classes would look to shops if they wanted some expensive textiles. They preferred the comfortable environment offered by the 'smarter' shop where they could get credit and other services.

This growing delight in 'shopping', particularly at the top of the social hierarchy, not only brought about a great increase in the available facilities to meet consumer demand but also fed a conspicuous consumption, particularly in the changing demand for clothing. Goods like dress and furniture formed an increasingly larger proportion of the wealth of the landed classes. But such eager consumption led inevitably to financial crisis for the aristocracy. Attempts were made to curb their extravagances and not only by the puritans. In Coventry, for example, the judicial authorities ruled that only citizens above the rank of sheriff, or whose goods were worth at least £100, could wear fur gowns, or satin and silk doublets. No wage labourer could wear velvet.

While this trend of conspicuous consumption was taking place, Coventry was shocked to find itself in a trade depression, all the more of a surprise because the period of growth that preceded it had been achieved so smoothly.

Before looking at the causes of this, let us look at the major reasons for this early growth, which had been two-fold. The town, which had begun in Anglo-Saxon and Norman times as a small agricultural community of several hundred persons living in a clearing on the south eastern fringe of the Forest of Arden, had developed rapidly because of its strategic location on roads and rivers. By the 13th century it had a gild structure, a political format and was a gathering place for foreign merchants. The other factor in its growth was its central position for ecclesiastical institutions, particularly the Benedictine monastery around which the town had sprung up. Leofric and his wife Godiva are said to have founded and funded this Benedictine Priory, and it was this, as much as her other activities, which led to the celebration of 'Dame Goodeyues Day', an annual affair for the Cappers. From small beginnings, the Priory became a huge and wealthy cathedral. Other religious orders also moved to Coventry because patrons offered them money to erect new buildings there.

These foundations spurred on the construction of such major architectual projects as St Michael's Church and St Mary's Gild Hall. The merchants of the town also financed a two-mile city wall that would have 20 towers and 12 gates. There were, therefore, plentiful supplies of wood, coal and building materials for use by the religious community.

To the south-east was a wealthy area of pasture, the Felden, which provided splendid grazing for sheep, and the wool they supplied could be easily transported on the road network to Leicester, Northampton, Chester, Worcester and, to the south, London, Southampton and Bristol. This farming area also produced ample barley, wheat and peas, while Warwickshire increasingly became known for its surpluses of corn, cheese and cloth. The religious institutions also supplied wool for Coventry's textile industry – indeed it was the expansion of the textile industry that turned the town over the years into a thriving medieval city. At first there was a busy trade in wool exports; later this shifted to exports of cloth.

By 1400, Coventry was not only a major centre for its traditional trade of marketing raw wool, but also the Midland's major clothing town. Many of its leading officials were wool dealers, and many of these were members of the Cappers and Mercers gilds. In 1450 there had not been a single capper in the city – yet a few years later it could be said that Coventry's chief trade was 'making round caps of wool'.

According to the chronicler Stowe (1525-1605) the earliest hats worn in medieval England were knitted, together with cloth hoods and some silk hats, all of which were the monopoly of the Cappers. In 1482 the Cappers and Hurers ('hure' is another word for a cap) presented a petition to Parliament complaining about the increasing use of machines in 'fulling' mills which thickened the cloth artificially. This led Parliament to forbid the practice – an example of the increasing state protectionism within the capping trade. The Victoria County History points out that most of the Acts concerned with clothing in Tudor times referred to caps. There were even price regulations – in Henry VIII's reign no hat could be sold above 20 pence and no knitted woollen cap over 32 pence, on pain of a fine of 40 shillings. However, in 1517 pardons were given to the following for breaking the law: – Richard Herynge, William Pysford, Richard Marlar, John Bagle, Humphrey Toucker, John Barneby, Richard Totty, John Stronge, Richard Kemsey, Richard Bunvey, John Swynneskoo, Richard Smyth, Henry Hynd, Henry Kylby, William Cotton and Joan Bryan (widow) – all cappers and hatters. Clearly the Cappers had

considerable political clout – perhaps because they were not merely a craft since, like merchants, they had to possess the capital to buy the wool and have it spun, knitted and fulled, as well as meeting the expenses involved in selling the finished article.

A bishop preaching at a fair, similar to those held in Coventry. The Cappers put on ceremonial attendances at such fairs for several centuries.

As has been noted, the city's fame rested particularly on the skill with which its weavers could turn out 'Coventry blue', a cloth which was woven, dyed and finished in the area. A document of 1382 names various types of cloth, ranging from the cheaper 'russets' sold at 5 pence a yard up to the most luxurious of all, the 'bluette'. This was the period when Coventry was embarking on its great textile expansion, earning its living in the luxury market. There was considerable cross-trading for export – Italians, for example, bought 'Coventry blue' in Southampton and London while bringing back from the Mediterranean woad, oil and madder (red dye). By the end of the 14th century, Coventry was producing more than six per cent of the nation's exports and, in the fiscal year 1397-8, more than 95 per cent of the total exported by the county. Records for the year 1400 show that The Drapery in Coventry's centre was dealing with the equivalent of 3,000 whole cloths a year, an output that represented some 6,000 working man-weeks. The place was full to the brim with stalls, booths and shops owned by members of the various gilds – Drapers, Mercers, and the like.

Trade expansion continued. In 1522, 83 cappers and hatters were working locally, and the Cappers was the largest single gild in the city. By the middle of century, more than 50 per cent of the town's master craftsmen were cloth workers, and by the end a gild of 24 master craftsmen was regulating the business. A decade later the Leet Court described the Capper's gild as 'now being in number many wealthy and honest persons'.

While the name 'capper' explains the growth of the woollen cap trade, as time went by the town also became famous for its thread, which by Elizabethan times was much in demand for embroidery, particularly for clothing for the nobility and the aspiring classes. 'Right Coventrie blue' thread had begun to be made about the year 1500, and some 50 years later a local man was noting that 'the Chiefest trade of Coventry was heretofore in making blue thread, and then the town was rich, even upon that trade only'. Dyers (who had their own gild by 1475) also

Dyeing was part of the processing of cloth, and 'Coventry blue' was one of the colours in greatest demand. Dyers had established their own gild by 1475.

became men of substance, as they too were merchants who must have sufficient capital to buy imported raw materials. The Mercers on the other hand were largely responsible for handling the wholesale and export trade of the Cappers. They dominated the upper echelons of the city throughout the 16th century until, with the extinction of their great families (the Pysfords, Marlers and Doddes) their days too were numbered.

Inevitably, as prosperity increased, the population exploded. From a village of a few hundred people Coventry reached 5000 inhabitants by 1280; one hundred years later the number was probably something between 7000 and 9000. By 1434 the population of Coventry may have reached 10,000, of which one third was in the wool and weaving trade. Then, suddenly, in the early 1500s, the population began to diminish and so did the city's prolonged economic growth. Historians give several reasons for this, though few of them are agreed as to the major factors in the decline. At the time, while writers recorded the facts, they seem curiously short on causes. In 1523 John Leland, for example, wrote 'the town rose by makying of cloth and capps, that now decayenge, the glory of the city decayethe'.

Probably the factor which had been so essential to Coventry's growth – its geographic position – was in turn one reason for its decline, but little could be done to alleviate the disadvantages of such an inland position. Being located centrally mitigated against much long-distance trade. A stagnating population in the rural areas also affected urban growth because it depressed the market for agricultural commodities, even though its purpose was to encourage a transfer to wool production. Landlords evicted husbandmen to make way for sheep, and village populations decreased – with Warwickshire one of the fiercest-hit areas. Between 1450 and 1520 many villages in the area disappeared entirely, the worst years being those around 1480.

By the early years of the 16th century, the agricultural slump had begun to slacken off – but just at this point the centrepiece of the city's prosperity, the manufacture of wool broadcloth, itself contracted rapidly. Historians are not agreed about the reason for this. One of them who has studied the subject in detail, Charles V. Pythian-Adams, cites declining overseas markets for cloth and restrictive gild practices in Coventry which 'stamped the enterprise on which trade and industry had flourished'. This crisis in the cloth trade, the plagues, the emigration of labour to the countryside – these were the factors which in his opinion 'shook the medieval city to its very foundations'.

HABILLEMENT DE L'HOMME
CHAPEAUX

MANUFACTURE FRANÇAISE
D'ARMES ET CYCLES DE SAINT-ETIENNE (Loire)
Maisons à PARIS *(42, rue du Louvre)*, MARSEILLE, LYON, BORDEAUX, LILLE, TOULOUSE, NANTES, ROUEN, NANCY, TOURS

Henry VIII's dissolution of the monasteries may also have reduced trade from pilgrims. In 1538-9 the court suppressed Coventry's major religious institutions, even though these had already to an extent become impoverished. Certainly at the time, city officials believed the King's action had done major damage to the town. An historian writing half a century later claimed that 'many thousands of the inhabitants, to seek

The growth of the industry in Europe may have been a significant factor in the decline of the manufacture of wool broadcloth in Coventry.

better lively-hoods, were constrained to forsake the city'. Dormer Harris says that by the middle of the 16th century the cappers had begun to feel the depression following on the issue of base money, which marked the later years of the reign of Henry VIII. Foreign caps, too, appeared as competition, although in 1511 it was forbidden to anyone below the rank of a knight to wear them; a later statute (1529) proscribed anyone even of the upper classes from spending more than two shillings on an imported cap or bonnet. Also the superior fashions of London, brought into the country by the omnipresent pedlar, seem to have tempted customers away from the provincial maker. One of the persons in Hales' *Dialogue of the Commonweal*, which refers to the Coventry of 1549, speaking of those who cannot be content to have 'cap, coat, doublet, hose, or shirt made in his country, but they must have their gear from London', adds that by this means 'the artificers of our towns are idle', while the merchant and capper in the *Dialogue* speaks lugubriously of the high prices and the ill effect they have upon his trade.

> 'Wherefore', he says, 'many of my occupation and other like heretofore have died rich men and been able to leave... some notable bequest for some good deed, as to make a bridge, to repair highways... or buy some lands to help the poor beginners of the occupation; yea, sometime they had such superfluity as they could over such bequests leave another portion to find a priest or to found a chantry in some parish church. And now we are scarce able to live without debt or to keep any servants at all, except it be a prentice or two, and therefore the journeymen, being forced to be without work, are the most part of these rude people that make these uproars abroad.'

Henry VIII's son, Edward VI, also attempted to prohibit the import of foreign caps or hats to protect the home industry. Those who were caught smuggling were fined 40 shillings – half to go to the king and half to the informer.

In 1570, in order to revive the languishing trade in this unmodish headgear, whose makers, it was said, had been brought to beggary by recent changes in fashion, Elizabeth's Parliament laid down that every male person of above seven years old not possessed of a rental of 20 marks a year,

Hats like those favoured by Rembrandt in the 17th century had been flooding the English market for nearly 100 years, despite protectionist legislation.

should wear on the Sunday or holy day a cap of wool wrought in England, under penalty of a fine of 3s.4d. This was the 'Statute cap' of *Love's Labours Lost*. 'Better wits have worn plain Statute caps', Shakespeare says, and it is ironic that the poet's uncle, Henry Shakespeare, was fined for not observing the law in this particular in 1583. It is probable that the efforts of the Coventry Cappers helped to bring about the passing of this Act, as there are entries in the Accounts Book about this time of presents of £4 and a cap made to Edmund Brownell, one of the Members of Parliament for the City. But while the lower classes were compelled to wear plain 'Statute caps', the fashionable indulged in headgear of rich velvet, taffeta, or a fine soft silk made in uncouth shapes, some 'perking up', according to Stubbs, 'like a steeple, some broad and flat, like the battlements of a house'.

More of the elaborate hats worn by Rembrandt for the self-portraits painted in his Amsterdam studio. They illustrate the competition faced by the English manufacturers in domestic and export markets.

The craft gilds of pre-Reformation times made it their business to limit competition between members, to keep alive a brotherly spirit, to provide for religious services on behalf of the dead, and to regulate questions of labour and workmanship. This last item was particularly insisted upon by outside authority, such as the Leet Court, which again and again laid down that caps were not to be flocked (i.e. thickened with wool dust). The number of apprentices was limited to two by the rules of 1496, both because apprentices were potential competitors and also because any master employing a larger number could execute more work than his fellow craftsmen. This jealousy of potential members and competitors extended to the 'foreigner' or stranger. The Doctor in Hales' *Dialogue* urges that encouragement should be given to skilful foreigners to settle in English towns, citing Venice and Norwich as examples of cities made rich by the incoming of skilful foreign workmen. 'But', he says,

> 'where other cities do allure unto them good workmen, our
> men will expel them out. As I have known good workmen, as
> well smiths as weavers, have come up from strange parties to
> some cities within the realm, intending to set up their crafts,
> and because they were not free there, but specially because
> they were better workmen than was any in the town, they
> could not be suffered to work there. Such incorporation had
> those misteries in those towns, that none might work there
> in their faculty except they did compond with them first.'

The Doctor's dictum is immediately answered by the Capper,
who wishes to know whether he thinks it reasonable that 'a stranger
should be as free in a city or town as they that were 'prentice there'.
'Then no man', he continues, 'would be 'prentice to any occupation if
it were so.'

Those citizens who remained in Coventry looked round for someone
to blame for their troubles. One group that became a target for abuse
was the fullers. Their art was indispensible to the clothmaker –
'fulling, rowing or teazling of cloth' to which might be added
stretching. In 1549 Archbishop Latimer preached a sermon before
Edward VI in which he censured those who stretched cloth and had
'a pretty feat to think him again [after] stretching. He makes me a
powder for it and plays the poticary; they call it flock powder. [But]
these mixtures come of covetousness. They are plain theft.'

Alas, abusing the fullers did not end Coventry's problems.
The manufacture of blue thread was the next activity to be hit. It
plummeted between 1553 and 1600. Local officials blamed this on
local dyers who used inferior methods, and on tradesmen in London
and Manchester who boosted their sales by pretending their ribbon

was 'Made in Coventry' and so counterfeited the Coventry brand.

The final blow came when the Cappers' trade, the largest employer and the mainstay of the town's prosperity, itself went into depression. Early in Elizabeth's reign the Leet Book records the reasons for, and the effects of, this depression. Before that date nearly all classes wore knitted wool caps, but when emigrés from Bruges and Normandy settled in England and began making and selling hats made of felt, the woollen cap quickly became unfashionable and sales plummeted. Other materials came into fashion too, notably caps of silk, velvet and other finery. There were complaints from the trade that these new cloths were 'causing the impoverishment and decay of great multitudes making woollen caps.... bringing good cities and towns to desolation'. As noted, legislation was introduced prohibiting the importation of foreign hats, but this had little effect. In desperation, the gild persuaded the politicians to insist that wool hats must be worn on 'special' days, but again the result was minimal. As early as 1533 a former city sergeant reported 'a great decay in this Citie for that Landie Craftsmen be not sette on work as they have been in tymes past, for the Citizens were wont to liff by the Craftes of Clothemaking, Cappyng, hatmakyng, not other occupacions'. In the same year another writer commented that 'ther is little maid ware or none but such as cometh from beyonde the See'. By the close of the decade, businesses had shut down, markets and fairs were empty, citizens were emigrating, property had decayed and trade seemed at a standstill.

Opposite: The Cappers' Accounts and Order Books survived the bombing of Coventry in World War II and provide a useful record of centuries of social and business life. This page in typical Georgian hand dates from 1772 when handwriting had become easier for the modern reader to decipher.

The Cappers' problems were not short-lived. On 17 August 1565, when

The Accompt of Mr. Henry Yardley Master and Mr. William Love Warden of the Company and Fellowship of Cappers and Feltmakers in the City of Coventry made and given up the twenty day of February 1772 in the twelfth Year of the Reign of our Sovereign Lord George the third by the Grace of God of Great Britain France and Ireland King Defender of the Faith and so forth And in the Year of our Lord 1772. Then being Mayor Mr. Jos: Cranor

The Members Names

Receipts of 1771.

		£	s	d
Mr. John Lowke				
James Birch Esquire	Rec'd of Mr. Worcester the Ballc:	5	12	4½
Mr. Cater Love	of his Acco't last Year			
Mr. Tho: Chapman	1. Jan'y 1772. Rec'd of Mr. Jos:	10	0	0
Mr. Tho: Little	Worcester 10 for one Years Rent	15	12	2½
Mr. Edw: Love	due at Michaelmas 1771			
Mr. James Jones				

Payments of 1771.

		£	s	d
Mr. Jos: Worcester		3	0	0
Mr. Hen: Yardley	28 Jan'y 1771. Paid for the Com'n Dinner	0	1	0
Mr. William Love	Paid for Opening the Church Door	0	11	8
Walter Waring Esqr.	Paid for Wine & Serv'ts 5/0	1	1	0
Sr. Rich: Glynn Baro:	Paid the Summoner's Salary	0	5	0
Mr. Samuel Payne	P. the Clerks D'o due Michaelmas 1771	0	16	4
Mr. Henry Smith	Paid Mr. Dakin Carpenters Bill	1	11	6
Mr. John Gibbs	Paid Mr. Chapman Jun'r	0	15	9
Mr. Tho: Butlin	Paid Mr. Worcester	0	3	8
Mr. Tho: Banbury	Pe. due one Years Seat Rent	1	19	9
Mr. Rich: Bird	P'd Freeth Colon's Bill 15.3 Allow'd 4/6	0	10	0
	Paid for Tiles & Sand	0	5	6
	Paid Mr. Chapman Sen'r	0	2	6
	Paid T. Nippcott Oakens Gift	11	3	8
	Paid for Ingrossing this Acco	0	1	6
	Total Payments L	11	4	2

	£	s	d
Total Receipts of 1771	15	12	2½
Total Payments of 1771	11	15	8
Balance due to the Com'n	3	16	0½

	£	s	d
Total Paym'ts	11	4	2
Mr. Adams's Bill	0	11	6
L	11	15	0

Elizabeth I passed through the town, the Recorder, John Throgmorton, interrupted his speech on the town's splendid history to comment on its present 'lamentable ruin and decay'.

Despite its shortcomings, Coventry must have had an appeal for Queen Elizabeth, for she returned the following year for three days, the 17th, 18th and 19th August 1566, accompanied by a huge retinue. She gave the city barely a month's warning of her arrival and lodged at the former house of the Whitefriars. Many gilds volunteered to perform dramatic works for her, but only four were chosen. The Cappers were not selected, but they assisted the Weavers to produce an ambitious tableau of St John's vision in the Book of Revelations when he saw the seven churches of Asia.

Priceless medieval records were stored in the Birmingham Free Library, which unfortunately was burnt down in 1878. That loss was nearly as bad as that 60 years later when the Germans bombed Coventry. The Cappers' records have survived in their two volumes, but all their other artifacts were destroyed. Other gilds whose written records survive include the Carpenters (Account Books and Ordinances), Cordwainers (Ordinances), Corvisors or Curriers (Accounts), Drapers (Accounts and Ordinances), Fullers (Ordinances), Mercers (Ordinances and Accounts; Minute Book), Tanners (Minute Book), Weavers (Account Books and Ordinances).

CHAPTER IV

'PAGEANTS AND DUTIES'

The previous chapters have attempted to survey the broad picture of medieval England, and middle England in particular. Now we turn more specifically to Coventry itself, and those of its citizens who were members of the major trade gilds. Historians believe that such citizens, described in modern terms as 'status groups', were bound to each other by highly developed occupational ties (such as the production of and trade in wool) plus – using another modern term – urban rituals such as mystery play performances, all of which combined to build a cohesive civil community, cross-linked by marriages and apprenticeships in the fellow trades. Indeed one historian says that the binding factor of a craft gild was its secret character; it was a 'mystery' (this word was used to describe a trade also) to be maintained by its initiates alone. He quotes in support the Cappers who were expressly forbidden

> 'to disclose nor utter no thyngs that ought of Right to
> be secretly to be kept amonges themselfes wherby any
> dyssension or debate might Ryse there uppon'.

It is not surprising, therefore, that membership of the craft gild provided one of the surest avenues to true status in the community. There was a 'cradle-to-the-grave' inevitability about this – nearly one in two of the members progressed to the officer class. It was 'nothing less than a transforming process [which] related the life cycle of

These four monks are a Victorian
reconstruction of the following orders
(clockwise from top left) Carthusian,
Benedictine, Franciscan and Carmelite.
The two religious fraternities in the
city were the Holy Trinity gild (1364)
and Corpus Christi (1350); senior
citizens aspired to membership
of both.

the citizen to the urban social system as a whole', says one historian. This process had been a continuing one in England since the early days of Coventry as a city – craft gilds had appeared as a recognised social unit before 1400, when Richard II gave a licence to the Shearmen and Tailors gild – what we should now call the Tailors and Cutters.

It is not suggested that the craft gild replaced religion in Coventry's social pattern. True, the great Benedictine monastery had declined by the late 15th century, but in the city itself there were Carmelites and Franciscans and outside the walls a charterhouse. Coventry's minster piously preserved in a case of copper and gilt the head of the martyred virgin Osburg who, being widely venerated in the Midlands, was the object of regional pilgrimage and subject of a brisk tourist trade.

Two great socio-religious fraternities co-existed inside the city walls, the gilds of Holy Trinity (1364) and Corpus Christi (1350), the latter being the junior of the two in status. For a citizen who wished to aspire to social eminence it was greatly desirable to be a member. Membership of these two gilds was in theory open to anybody, but in practice it was limited by the high entrance fee and the cost of livery. There appears to be an acceptance that membership should be confined to the more distinguished members of crafts. On the other hand there is some evidence that from early times some citizens who were not practicing the capper trade were accepted into gild membership.

The Cappers, like other gilds, were headed by the masters of the craft, and in 1520 nearly half the craftsmen (282 out of some 600) were also members of Corpus Christi and hoped to be translated in due course to Holy Trinity, which had a substantial income from its many properties. Of the 25 Cappers who were amongst the wealthiest members of their fellowship, some 21 joined the gild of Corpus Christi. They included the future élite of the city. For example, of the seven Cappers whose career profiles can be followed through the years 1500-50, all achieved the considerable position of sheriff. As such, they would have had active religious as well as secular duties to perform.

The Cappers' own chapel was in St Michael's Church. The Mercers and Drapers had their own chapels there, as did the Dyers. In 1590 the Mercers moved to St Mary's Gild Hall. The most ancient part of the church structure is the south porch, restored in mid-Victorian times. In this area was the Cappers' Room and above the chapel where the gild formerly held its meetings. Both were damaged in the great air raids of World War II. For many years it was, it is said, 'a dingy neglected place', though restored in 1860 at the same time as the porch, with a new stained-glass window added, bearing the arms of the gild. Opposite is a window giving a view of the church. It may have been the site of a tomb of some dignitary. A plaque on the walls records earlier repairs:

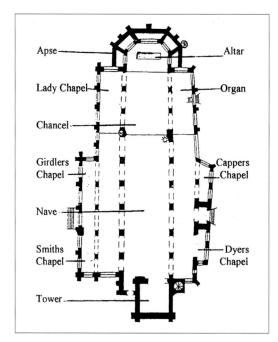

A plan of St Michael's Church as it was before the German bombing, showing the position of the Cappers' and other gild chapels.

When the chapel was restored in 1860, a new stained-glass window was added, bearing the arms of the gild (left) as well as those of the city (right).

'This chapell was repaired anno domini 1666, then being masters of the fellowship of Cappers and Feltmakers, Mr Abraham Owen and Mr William Quinborough... this chappell was repaired and the pews built anno domini 1726, then being masters of the fellowship of Cappers and Feltmakers Mr Thomas Smith and Mr Samuel Tompson.'

One of the Victorian histories of Coventry says that St Thomas's Chapel, which joins the south porch eastward, was the original Cappers' chapel, and in 1629 there arose a dispute with the church-wardens which resulted in a commutation of the gild's rights to use this chapel, which was reduced to six seats only, for each

of which they had to pay four pence annually. Another history, while not specifically referring to a dispute, says the Cappers surrendered their chapel to the parish in 1629 for the sum of £15. The chamber over the porch, which has retained the name Cappers' Chapel, was reached by a winding stair and used for annual meetings on St Thomas's Day. Dormer Harris describes it as 'a small furnished room with a chimney piece made of the lid of a stone coffin

A photograph from the Dormer Harris book of 1921 showing the entrance to the chapel, later destroyed in the bombing.

bearing a floriated cross'. That there was always some problem or dispute about the Cappers' title to the chapel is clear from an 1874 Order authorising a deputation to discuss the matter with the Vicar.

In addition to worshipping in the Cappers' chapel, it seems that the fraternity also attended the cathedral for the commemorative mass for the founders of the Priory, Leofric and Godiva. Entries in the Accounts Book before the Reformation record offerings of 10 pence on these occasions.

While a Capper's trade was the modest one of making up knitted or woven caps or repairing them and keeping them in good order, his 'official' duties within the gild were more elaborate. For example when the Capper Nicholas Heynes became Mayor in 1525 there was a Cappers' festivity at Candlemas for which he may have borne the expense. This included 6s. 8d. for the 'soteltyes', or 'subtletys', a feast dish of fanciful shape and rich ornamentation. Decorating these cost an extra eight pence. Other duties were civic or political because the gild, as well as looking after the well-being of its members, also acted as a channel of communication with local and central government.

In fact the gild was the unit of industrial organisation which operated through the Leet Court, some of whose officers were in turn gild members. In order to execute its wishes, the Leet would appoint 'searchers'. These men would, amongst other duties, examine both the cloth and the equipment used to produce the finished articles to ensure they came up to standard. In turn, the Leet also appointed drapers to see that the searchers did their work conscientiously. The Leet Book makes it clear that they did so. It is recorded, for example, that certain cappers were fined after being found guilty of flocking their cloth. On the other hand, if the cloth was good, it was sealed with the Coventry city arms.

'Bad' cloth could still be sold, but without the seal of approval.

So what was it like to be a Capper in 16th-century Coventry? The years 1496-1550 saw 'the take-off and meteoric rise' of the capping industry – the number of 'masters' having apprentices and journeymen rising from 25 to 70 over this period. They represented, nevertheless, a mere 10 per cent of the towns' tradesmen, though one of their number, John Dove, was elected Mayor of Coventry, the first time a Capper had achieved this eminence. He was followed by Thomas Padland or Patlond (1504), John Saunders (1510), Nicholas Heynes (1525) and Hugh Lawton (1533).

These achievements could not disguise the fact that the Cappers were seen as essentially *nouveau riche* at the beginning of the century; they held a modest place in the pecking order of crafts or trades. Indeed the historian Pamela King says that the gild's growing affluence was based not upon long hours of hard effort so much as on its ability to put out work to cheap labour to meet what we would call the niche-marketing demands of the fashion business. The most senior company was the Mercers, which included Grocers, Vintners and some Cappers – the latter did not separate off until the 1490s. Second in importance was the Drapers, then the once-proud Dyers, followed by the Weavers. The Fullers may have split into the two groups, Weavers and Cappers, as their ordinances were not admitted until 1496. There were six leather trades: Skinners, Whittawers, Glovers, Tanners, Corvisors and Saddlers. The latter joined with the Cardmakers. Another six were in the food trades, five in the metal trades, four in building crafts, the 'arms industry' of Bowers and Fletchers (amalgamated), and the Barbers and Ropers.

Later, the order changed again, and by 1522 the Shearmen

and Tailors were the biggest craft, closely followed by the Cappers, outstripping the Mercers, Drapers and Weavers. The Fullers had only 20-30 members. These figures do not necessarily reflect the numbers of people working at a craft, as a 1522 survey makes clear.

Membership of leading occupations in a survey of 1522

Cappers	83
Weavers	41
Shearmen	38
Butchers	36
Shoemakers	28
Drapers	28
Dyers	28
Bakers	27
Mercers	26
Tailors	21
Tanners	15
Smiths	14

Despite this relative numerical inferiority of 83:28, the Drapers are described as 'the foremost entrepreneurial trading company compared with the Cappers and Weavers'. The Drapers had, it is said, broken the Dyers' monopoly and recruited several smaller other gilds which traded in the premises known as The Drapery, situated near Jordan Well, off Earl Street. Another function of The Drapery was to house cloth which had to be inspected and given the seal of approval. Lists were kept there of the makers of cloth 'approved' by the inspectors. The Drapers, who administered The Drapery, had 'searchers' who inspected the cloth both morning and afternoon, looking carefully for defects. Those that passed the test were fixed with a lead seal; they were also weighed. Rejected or defective cloth was fixed with a cannulation seal. In this way, the quality was kept up, as approval was only given to cloth that was heavy, glossy and perhaps glowing with a soft blue dye. The cloth was then exported or, perhaps, made up by the cappers for headgear for the home market.

The Cappers' comparatively lowly place in the social pecking order was to some extent related to their choice of geographic location. Like the butchers, the Cappers had a concentrated occupational grouping, largely centred on the Jordan Well ward, though it overlapped into neighbouring areas and even went as far afield as Spon Street ward. These two wards ranked towards the bottom of the scale in terms of the rental value of their properties. Nearly half the properties were 'working-class' housing; Jordan Well, with 60 per cent, was bottom of the housing league.

Evidence for the activities of the Cappers gild appears not only in their own documentation but, along with that of other 'craft' gilds, can be found in the City's Leet Book, where those who ran the city – the mayor and his colleagues – recorded their decisions, Coventry is fortunate in having such a record, covering the years 1421-1555, in a massive volume, bound in board and leather, with handwritten entries.

The Leet Court met twice a year, at Easter and Michaelmas, to frame ordinances grounded on petitions presented by the folk of the city to the mayor. It was primarily a local court of justice (other examples have been found at Norwich, Manchester and Southampton) which could execute summary punishment on thieves or on those who cheated the consumer by selling false measures of food or drink.

No witnesses were usually called – the Court routinely relied on the facts presented to it. Fines were enforced by the bailiffs, who made a levy on the possessions of the transgressor. (See page 49 for details of the searchers' duties.)

In 1496 the Master and Fellowship of the Cappers Company had brought their book of ordinances to the Leet for confirmation; amongst the orders they wished to have approved were the following:

(1) Masters were not to employ more than two apprentices and were to keep them indentured for not less than seven years.

(2) Their journeymen were not to make caps on their own account, but only for their masters, though they might repair old bonnets.

(3) Wages were fixed and no strangers were to be employed without licence from the master.

(4) No member of the craft was to teach any part of his trade to anyone except his apprentices or his wife.

A journeyman was a qualified craftsman who had completed his apprenticeship and then continued to work regularly for his master for a daily wage. Each master was allowed two apprentices only, and there were to be no replacements without licence from the Leet. The apprentices in turn had to pay their masters to teach them the skills of the trade. In 1496 the sum required was 13s. 4d. on 'setting up' if the apprentice was a 'native'. Strangers had to pay twice that amount. Too much can perhaps be read into these Leet ordinances, according to Pamela King, who claims that the Cappers were a *parvenu* gild 'struggling throughout the late 15th and early 16th centuries to achieve recognition'.

The housing of the cappers has been briefly described, and like most other craftsmen of the period their working environment too was relatively harsh. The medieval day extended for 12-14 hours but was broken by set times for meals, usually provided by the masters. There was half an hour for breakfast, an hour for 'dinner' and half an hour for 'noon-meat'. In the summer a siesta was allowed. Throughout the year, journeymen cappers did not finish work until 7pm, sometimes an hour earlier. Most of Saturday was a working day except for those attending at the market, but it finished early – cappers were forbidden to mill caps 'on the Saterday after evunsong' (about 4pm) 'nor the Sonday tyle evunsong be don' after which they could do so. Saturday was pay day.

Apprentices and journeymen cappers mostly worked at their masters' premises, and in 1520 they were only permitted to 'freshe and scower old Bonettes in ther own howsys'. An apprenticeship with the (middling) crafts of Weavers, Cappers and Hatmakers was a seven-year stint. If there was trouble, the apprentice was given notice, usually a week, though the Cappers extended this to two weeks in 1520. It seems clear the men did not set up shop till they were married – and weddings were usually late. As for the master Cappers, the bachelors among these seem to have been married within at most four years of setting up shop. Their weddings were attended by all the other master Cappers; absence attracted a fine.

The Cappers' records suggest that on average a man's working life was over by the time he was 40, or at most 50. On the death of her husband, the widow of a capper was expected to carry on the family business until her children went out to service. Such widows were called – in the Capper's Accounts – 'goodwives'. In some cases a 'goodwife' could take over from a sick husband before he died – paying his 'quarterage' fee to the Cappers from the earlier date. In the case of cappers and weavers, widows were not expected to take on apprentices themselves.

So while women had a practical part to play in the cappers' trade – particularly in the early days when spinners and knitters were exclusively women – it was by and large a male-dominated fraternity. It was also what the historians call a gerontocratic system, that is one ruled by the elderly. Thus, while one history suggests that this kind of craft gild came about because the young journeymen had a hankering for gratification in the same kind of 'merry meetings and feasts' indulged in by their elders and betters who had formed the so-called religious gilds some 40-50 years earlier, the senior citizens soon took over the craft gilds too. It is suggested that the city fathers supported such gilds because they provided an instrument through which to regulate the economic and the social life of the city.

Though the craft gilds' main purpose was economic, because they combined the common interests of the same craft or 'mystery', the religious element was not far away. Plays and the pageants are spoken of as early as 1416, and a pageant house even earlier, in 1392, so plays may have been in existence well before that. Indeed, it is claimed that the Coventry mystery plays go back to the days of the Franciscan foundation. Pamela King believes that the Cappers' acquisition of a Corpus Christi pageant was central to their striving ambition for recognition in the city, mentioned earlier. Indeed they became, she says, major players in the pageant cycle at a time when the cycle itself was in its closing stages. More will be said about the plays and pageant houses later, but here it is interesting to note that one of the Cappers who became a senior officer in the fellowship was Robert Crowe. He is one of the most frequently mentioned players, though Pamela King says we cannot be sure if he is one man or several with the same name. In 1510 a Robert Crowe is admitted brother of the Cappers gild, and pays 20 pence in fees each year until 1515-6, when his membership dues are paid off. In 1513-4 a Robert Crowe is involved in a lawsuit with the gild, but in 1520 was Master. In 1522 he took on an apprentice and appears to have lived in Baileylane Ward. The historian Halwin, an expert on the pageants, thinks he is the Crowe who married Joyce Botiler in 1532-3, and who may then have given up capping because she brought money into the marriage.

This is the point at which Crowe the theatrical impresario appears on the scene; we know that as early as 1525 he had masterminded an extravagant Candlemas celebration for the Cappers called 'Golden Fleece'. His name appears on the gild records twice – once being paid eight pence by the Cappers for the 1540 Corpus Christi Day expenses (it was the height of social standing to perform a Corpus Christi Day pageant) and later, in 1547, two shillings for mending Herod's head, mitre and 'other things'.

From this period Crowe is always associated with plays, but he worked for many different gilds. He wrote the Shearmen and Tailors' and the Weavers' playbooks in 1535, and they paid him 20 shillings for a new one in 1557. He also worked for the Smiths, and played God for the Drapers in 1562 and '66. They gave him a special reward for his efforts. His work for the Drapers also became more regular thereafter. He made 'worlds' that they burned in 1556, 1561, 1563 and 1566, as well as two 'giants' for their 1556 midsummer show. Another historian, H. Craig, suggests he became a sort of script-writer and staff manager of the Corpus Christi plays.

In the 1530s the Cappers had just taken over a pageant, but none of their records survive for the period when this Capper, Crowe, was working most actively for the Drapers. However he left behind two scripts, one his holograph copy.

The city council controlled these entertainments rigidly, and when some craft gilds found them to be a burden and tried to drop them, the council forced them to continue, claiming that they brought trade and prestige to the city. The Drapers and Mercers were wealthy enough to continue, but the Hatmakers joined with the Mercers to share the expense of putting on plays and pageants.

A pageant was strictly speaking a moveable vehicle which served as a stage,

An imaginative reconstruction of a pageant or mystery play. The Cappers began this important civic activity after 1531, and there are details of its 'programme' of scenes from Corpus Christi Day in 1534.

and this had to be stored, when not in use, in a 'pageant house'. Now, the Cappers had originally contributed to the Girdlers' pageant but during the early 16th century they were in such a flourishing state that in 1531 they asked the Leet if they could have their own chapel. The Leet agreed, commenting that the Cappers 'now beying in nomber meny welthy and honest persones' well deserved this distinction. Since the Cardmakers and Saddlers were on hard times, the Cappers joined them at St Thomas's Chapel in St Michael's Church, which, within six years, they had completely taken over for their own use. At one time they had the Tailors' pageant house in Mill Lane, shared with the Weavers and Tailors, and they would perhaps have taken over the Weavers' pageant had the latter not, with the assistance of the Walkers, managed to hang on.

Most of the gilds met for social purposes three times a year, though the Cappers' practice was to meet only twice. The 'choice dinner' was in the summer time, representing the old meeting day of St Anne or the Name of Jesus. The Account Feast took place in December, January or February, representing the old Cardmakers' Feast of the Translation of St Thomas. The following items of expenses at such a feast day occur on the first page of the Accounts Book:

In primis, paid at the first quarterage

In bread	12d.
Item, in servicia [ale]	18d.
Item, in 'chekenes'	7d.
Item, paid for 12 anes [sic? ducks] ..	2s 8d.
Item, paid for flour to the bake meats ..	12d.
Item, paid for beef and lamb in the shambles	3s 6d.
Item, paid for spices ..	2s 2d.
Item, paid for vinegar and salt and mustard	2d.
Item, paid for frummetty and milk ..	4d.
Item, paid for fuel and coals	5d.
Item, paid for hire of vessell and broches [spits]	3d.
Item, paid for the oven	6d.
Item, paid for butter	2d.
Item, paid to the scullions, turn-broches [turnspits]	2d.
Item, paid to the cook and his servant ..	6d.

A very usual entry is a payment to musicians, such as

Paid to the minstrel on Jesus day ..   12d.

The Cappers had other social gatherings. For example it was their duty to maintain the archery butts outside the city walls (the street called Barkers' Butts still survives) and one of the records shows that the fellowship paid the costs involved when their members met to carry out their butt duties in Little Park.

Each fellowship usually had two officers, though the Drapers and Mercers each had four. The Cappers, in addition, had several Wardens to look after their 'lands'. Such officers were usually drawn from Masters who had set up shop over the past decade, and the move to a senior position would take 14-15 years – hence the accuracy of the term 'gerontocracy'. There were lesser officers – a summoner and a clerk – to arrange their meetings and keep their records.

The major reason for the Cappers' decline – the growth of feltmaking – has been noted in a previous chapter. As capping was 'decayenge, so the glorie of the city decayethe, too'. Cries of woe were heard and not only in Coventry. Other centres like Bristol, Chester, Gloucester and Lichfield felt the rot, though perhaps not over as long a period. Despite this decline, membership of the Coventry gild held up well, the lowest period in its fortunes being reached much later when the transition to feltmaking was complete.

Records for the period from 1497-8 to 1539-40 show that during that time some 33 Cappers held senior office in their gild and of these as many as six moved on to become junior officers of the city council. Another six went on to become sheriffs and Nicholas Heynes was mayor for a short term around 1525. Mayors had social as well as political duties, and their hospitality was sometimes on a grand scale. At least one mayor kept open house for the full twelve days of Christmas. Others provided drink for their journeymen, and new mayors and craft officers financed a meal for their new members at the time of inauguration. However, by 1566, a mere 26 names are listed in the Accounts, only one of these having the trade description 'hats, caps and trimmings thereof'.

There was a good deal of social mobility, apprentices becoming masters and in due course officers of the gild, perhaps then moving on to city office. Journeyman Cappers (according to the records) were not so quick to mount the ladder of office. Indeed, only about one third of those who enrolled became masters at all, and only one achieved craft office in the first half of the century. Masters themselves, as already indicated, were keen to hold office – or, at least, some of them were. Of the 42 who held senior office before 1554-5, some 15 held office a second time, of whom eight had been sheriff. There was, it seems, no family 'monopoly' – in the 60-year period before 1554-5, only two families were involved in senior office through successive generations.

Berger, writing about the Mercers, gives a picture which presumably would not differ greatly for the Cappers. Tradesmen who entered city politics, where competition for the top offices was even more intense than in the gild itself, he says, all went through the *'cursus honorum'* – a series of gradually more responsible positions, with a fixed number of years between offices. In addition to minor posts in the ward and the parish, men could hold up to six major offices in Coventry. The first step was warden or chamberlain; no one held both offices. Then it was normal to move on to the Leet Court, then to the sheriff's office, then to the council where they usually remained until near to the end of their lives. Finally a few successful tradesmen would become mayor. There was an average of 28 years between the first stage of becoming a freeman and the mayoralty. A few performed the journey much more quickly, perhaps in only 10 years – but they were a minority. If the Mercers are a pointer to the reasons for this, they are mainly two-fold:

(1) There were considerable expenses involved in holding high office

(2) The holder was prevented from devoting much time to his own business due to the demands of office. The latter would be much greater than the demands of gild office though these were not inconsiderable – collecting dues, seeing to gild properties, dispensing charity and keeping accounts.

A no less significant rôle must have been played by those Cappers who held the Sovereign's Letters Patent for the making of hats and caps. Early in Elizabeth's reign these had been granted to John Baylie and Robert Blunte, but for some reason were later called in; as a result, towards the end of the reign, in 1590, the Cappers petitioned for new patentees – Richard Smythe, Richard Barker, Thomas Whyte and Rafe Brown, all aldermen.

The Cappers took a much greater part in public life after 1531, when, as noted, they became associated with the Cardmakers and Saddlers, eventually taking over not only their Chapel of St Thomas in St Michael's Church, but also assisting the two less-well-off gilds with their pageant at the Feast of Corpus Christi. In 1533 they even went so far as to emulate London gilds by introducing a giant with a candle in his head which was the highlight of that year's midsummer show.

Dormer Harris quotes from records showing that each member of the united fellowship paid 12d. a year towards these expenses under this new arrangement, and gave 1d. at the offertory at the High Mass said in the chapel on the Feast of the Translation of St Thomas (29th December). 'Also', the record runs, 'it is enacted that the masters and company of the craft of Cappers shall from henceforth familiarly and lovingly accompany and sit together in the said chapel with the said company and craft of Cardmakers and Saddlers to hear their divine service and also shall go together in their processions and watches two and two together'.

The company of Cardmakers and Saddlers were to have 'the pre-eminence and overhand in their sitting and going together one year, and the said craft and company of Cappers shall likewise have the pre-eminence and overhand in their sitting and going another year, and so to continue from year to year lovingly from henceforth so that the said Cardmakers and Saddlers shall not lack their room and sitting in the said chapel'. In 1537, however, the Cardmakers withdrew from the united fellowship and surrendered their pageant and chapel entirely to the Cappers.

The indenture by which this conveyance was made is quoted in Sharp's *Antiquities of Coventry*, where there is a list of the jewels and ornaments belonging to the chapel. These included a Mass Book and a chalice, four sets of Eucharistic vestments, two pageant cloths of the Passion, a pax of Jesus, Mary and Peter (this was handed round to receive the kiss of peace), a pair of altar cloths with chrisms (a white cloth put on infants at the time of their baptism and worn for seven days), with other vestments and jewels, which were probably all sold at the Reformation.

A grand pall was evidently made in 1495, the cost of the stuff and the workmanship being entered on the first leaf of the accounts. Velvet for the ground of the pall and red velvet for the cross upon it, buckram to line it, silk for the fringe, and badges (bearing no doubt the company's emblems of the scissors and teasel) are all mentioned, though it would appear from the items that the original pall differed from the one that survived into the 20th century. This cross appeared to be in yellow velvet (not red), and there were seven shields, three with scissors of a different shape being placed rather carelessly and crookedly in various parts of the pall. It is possible that these three shields represented a fragment of the great pall of 1495, the remainder belonging to a later date. To judge from later entries, it was evidently repaired several times. Fourpence was paid 'for mending of our pall' in 1597.

In the accounts there are the various items connected with the making of this fine piece of needlework:

In primis, paid for 5 yards of velvet at 12s.6d. the yard.

Summa [sum total]	..	55s.8d.
Item, half a yard of red velvet [at] 10s. 3d. Summa		15s.4½d.
6 yards buckram at 6d. the yard. Summa	..	3s.0d.
Item, paid for 5 oz. silk in skeins and ribbon	..	5s.10d.
Item, paid for weaving of the fringe	..	10d.
Item, paid for stiff cloth	..	7d.
Item, paid for workmanship of the two badges and stuff	..	10s.0d.
Item, paid for finishing and making of the pall		13s.4d.
Item, paid for the coffer that the pall is in	..	18d.
Item, 2 oz. of ribbon and a quarter	..	2s.2d.
Sum total	..	£5 8s.3½d.

In addition to worshipping in the Cappers' chapel at St Michael's Church, the fraternity attended, it seems, at the Cathedral for the commemorative mass for the pious founders of Coventry Priory,

A grand pall was evidently made in 1495 but that above, photographed for the Dormer Harris history of 1921, may well have been of a later date. It is shown here hanging above the fireplace in the then Cappers' Room. However, it was destroyed along with other fine objects (listed in Sharp's *Antiquities*) in the 1940s' bombing raids. A modern replacement now hangs in the Cappers' Room.

Leofric and Godiva. A very usual entry before the Reformation relates to their offering on this occasion, such as:

Offered at Dame Goodyues masse Xd. (10d.)

or

Offered on dame Goodyuez daye XIIId. (13d.)

One scribe writes 'Godwyn day' or 'Gudwyn day' and the meaning may be 'Goodwife's Day', 10th September. We have no clue as to the particular day on which this service was held.

The subject of the pageant or play, usually religious, was written up and rehearsed. Though no text survives, we know that the subject of the pageant which the Cappers took from the Cardmakers and performed on the Feast of Corpus Christi, the day before Coventry Fair, from the year 1534, includes the Descent into Hell, the Resurrection, the Appearance to Mary Magdalene in the Garden, and to the Disciples at Emmaus. The stage properties (or props) included Hell-mouth, the Sepulchre, Pilate's Club – discovered by Sharp in 1790 – and the Devil's Head. The characters consisted of Pilate (a loud-voiced boaster), Christ, the mysterious Mother of Death, four Knights (soldiers guarding the Sepulchre), the Spirit of God, Our Lady (a part that disappears in the reign of Edward VI), two Bishops (Annas and Caiaphas, who appear with Pilate at the grave after the Resurrection), two Angels, Mary Magdalene, two other Maries, and the Demon. The cast certainly included Adam and Eve, since their apple tree is mentioned; they were drawn out of Hell by Christ.

The Cappers continued to perform their pageant down to 1546 when, as Dormer Harris notes, William Shakespeare would have been 16 years old. He would certainly have heard of 'Coventry's

For many years the Accounts Book gives the same kind of information, income (rents and fines) and payments (expenditure). Here in a page from 1664, the latter substantially exceed the former.

Another imaginative reconstruction of the pageant structure. Though involving them in considerable expense, the Cappers' performances immensely increased their prestige in the city pecking order.

plays', since these were so widely known that they became a generic name for mystery plays in general. For about a century and a half kings and nobles 'took great delight' in them. In 1457 Margaret of Anjou surrounded by courtiers nibbling green ginger, pippins, and 'two coffins of comfits' saw them performed outside the house of a local dignitary, where she was staying.

Richard III and Henry VII also saw the plays (Henry saw them twice) and royal visits were sometimes enlivened by special pageants written for the specific visitor. For example Margaret of Anjou was welcomed in 1456 by speeches from Isaiah, Jeremiah, St Edward and St John, as well as the four cardinal virtues. Prince Arthur, visiting Coventry in 1498, saw the Nine Worthies, and listened to speeches narrated by King Arthur and St George. When Princess Mary visited Coventry in 1526, her entertainment was more modest – she only saw the Mercers' pageant, probably because it featured the Assumption of Mary.

The Cappers would have had to find a considerable amount of money to finance these pageants. The moveable vehicles which served as stages had to be kept in a good state of repair and some of these two-storey 'pageants' were elaborately embellished with carved crests and gilt vanes, and hung with curtains. They had to hire premises for their rehearsals, and keep their costumes in repair. An item in the accounts for 3s. 4d. was 'spent at the Crane at the putting out of Pilate's doublet'. Refreshments had to be provided for the players and the pageant master.

Music was often an important part of the pageants. At Prince Edward's reception in 1474, the four pageants were accompanied by minstrelay 'of the waits of the city', 'of harp and dulcimer', 'of small pipes' and 'of organ playing'. The pageant to welcome Prince Arthur in 1498 included 'angels censing and singing, with organs and other melody'. Songs, like the well-known Coventry carol in the Shearmen and Tailors' pageant, were probably an integral part of most of the plays and there are payments for singers and musicians in the Accounts Books of the Cappers, Drapers, Smiths, Weavers, and Carpenters. The singers were often clerks and there were some independent minstrels, but most of the music was provided by the city waits – a company of wind instrumentalists paid for out of the public purse.

The earliest reference to the waits is an entry in the Leet Book under 1423, recording the appointment of four men as city minstrels and giving details as to their payment. The men were to have 'as others have had afore them'. They were paid by quarterage, a rate of 1d. from every hall and ½d. from every cottage each quarter. (Quarterage was not necessarily paid quarterly – it had now become a general item.) The Holy Trinity gild provided them with rent-free cottages, and they also received payment from the gilds and crafts for each occasion upon which they were hired. These included, besides playing in the pageants and processions on Corpus Christi Day, festivities on Midsummer Eve, and the annual feasts held by each gild. Any occasion calling for general rejoicing included the waits, from the reception of royalty to their triumphal procession. The waits must have been in demand throughout a wide area, for in 1467 a Leet order restricted them to within 10 miles of the city, unless high-ranking ecclesiastics should ask for them outside.

There were probably always four waits, the chief of whom was a trumpeter, and the rest played pipes, and probably drums and a stringed instrument – perhaps a dulcimer, later a violin. Organs and regals or small organs were favourite instruments in the 16th century. The waits wore the city's livery – coats or cloaks of green and red and silver escutcheons and collars or chains.

The antiquarian scholar Thomas Sharp (1770-1841), who incidentally was the son of a Coventry hatter, was a collector of items connected with the pageants. He discusses at length the club or 'mall' and the leather balls which were used by Pilate in the Cappers' pageant. A leather club believed to be the original prop, he personally discovered amongst the Cappers' effects, presumably in the early 1800's. Alas, none of these items survives.

As there is no detailed record of a specific Cappers' pageant or procession, it may be possible to give some impression of what it may have been like by taking the account given by H. Craig in his book *Corpus Christi Plays*. The Corpus Christi pageants were performed by the Mercers from 1579 until 1588, when they sold their pageant. The procession started early on the morning of Corpus Christi, with the crafts, dressed in livery, proceeding in twos, preceded by torch-bearers and attended by their journeymen. The senior company, the Mercers, came last, immediately before the Host, which was the special responsibility of Corpus Christi gild. Holy Trinity gild was also represented, its priest bearing equally valuable processional crosses, canopies and candlesticks. The mayor and civic dignitaries, probably robed in their scarlet and green gowns, armed guards and some of the principal actors also took part in the procession. The streets were decorated with boughs and noisy with the ringing of bells and the music of the waits. The plays were probably performed after the procession, the heavy pageants being dragged into position in places where there was enough space for the spectators and for performances which sometimes spilled over into the street. Gosford Conduit, Cross Cheaping, Little Park Street end, and one Richard Wood's house provided such stations, and it has been suggested that there were up to 10 stations, one for each ward.

Pageants and plays were not the only occasion for festivities – throughout the year there were many days set aside for jollity and communal feasts. The year began with the twelve days of Christmas, conducted by a Lord of Misrule. St George's Day on 23rd April and Hock Tuesday, the second Tuesday after Easter, were followed soon after by May Day. Most festivities fell in the summer – Corpus Christi on the Thursday after Trinity Sunday, then Midsummer Day and the Nativity of St John the Baptist on 24th June, St Peter's Day on 29th June and Lammas Day on 1st August. May Day involved the usual decoration of the streets and setting up of maypoles with accompanying rites. Hock Tuesday, which was originally celebrated by very primitive and boisterous customs, seems to have been turned into a play in 1416, representing the defeat of the Danes by the English. St Peter's Eve and Lammas Day were marked by feastings and ridings, in the case of the latter to open the common fields. But, apart from Corpus Christi, the biggest occasion was Midsummer Eve.

The Midsummer Eve torchlit procession, called a 'watch', involved the mayor and civic officials in scarlet and velvet robes, the city's armed guard, the crafts proceeding in the same order they observed in the Corpus Christi procession, bearing huge straw figures of giants which were probably burnt in the bonfires in which the celebrations culminated, just as straw giants are burnt today in Valencia. The streets were decorated with flowers and branches, mainly of birch, and there was much eating and drinking, although in 1545 the mayor and sheriffs were ordered to restrict their drinking to before the watch. Holy Trinity gild also held processions.

There were other occasions for communal feasting. Besides Midsummer Eve and St Peter's Eve, Holy Trinity gild celebrated the feasts of St John Lateran (6th May), the Trinity, the Decollation of St John (29th August), St Matthew (21st September), Michaelmas (29th September), and St Luke (18th October), as well as numerous obits. Corpus Christi held a Lenten dinner, a breakfast on the morning of Corpus Christi, a goose dinner in August and a venison dinner in October. In 1492 the gild spent £26 in feasts, only 13 shillings less than the annual stipend of its five priests. The craft gilds also enjoyed refreshment, both on special occasions like Corpus Christi Day, and after general meetings of the craft. The members of Holy Trinity gild consumed a variety of wines – white wine, 'wine of Tyre', claret, malmesey, sack and muscatel. The more prosperous craft gilds like the Dyers had red and white wine, but the most common drink of all was ale. St Mary's Hall was used for feasting not only by Holy Trinity gild but by some of the more important crafts, such as the Drapers and Mercers. Corpus Christi gild seems to have held its celebrations at St Nicholas's Church though it may have dined in Mill Lane as well. Other craft gilds hired rooms in one of the religious houses – Bablake, Greyfriars, and especially Whitefriars, but they probably also met in inns and alehouses, like the Gascoyne Tavern where the smiths met in 1468-71. The Cappers of course had their room in what is now St Michael's, and they meet to this day.

The Cappers, like some of the other gilds, had serious civic responsibilities as well as theatrical/religious ones. One of these occurred in 1543, when Henry VIII, made an expedition to France. The Cappers equipped three men. These are a few items out of the men's expenses:

Item, paid for the scouring of the harness .. 6d.

Item, paid for three men drinking at morning
    and at night .. 14d.

Item, paid for a 'zessternel' [gesteron = coat of mail] 10s.0d.

Item, paid for a pair of 'spellenttes' [= splints or pieces
    of armour to protect the elbow] .. 2s.8d.

Item, paid for a gorget [neck armour] .. 10d.

Item, paid for a sallet [helmet] .. 6s.0d.

Item, paid for three daggers .. 3s.0d.

Item, paid for bracers [protection for the arms]
    and shooting gloves .. 8d.

Item, paid for three pairs of boots .. 8d.

Item, paid for three night caps .. 10d.

Item, paid for their breakfast when they went forth 20d.

From the surviving Order Book of the Cappers gild it is clear that much of the pomp and ceremony was over by the end of the 16th century, although they still enjoyed processions when these were available. As noted, pageants were no longer actively performed after

1580, though twice (in 1584 and 1591) the Cappers contributed to another play, 'The Destruction of Jerusalem', which may have been more secular, and more suited to Protestant tastes.

From about 1600, the Accounts and Orders Books show that the main thrust of the Cappers' activities well in to the 17th century is on disciplinary measures. Most orders are concerned with the duties of masters and the restrictions placed on apprentices and journeymen – in today's jargon, with monopolistic practices. Great attention is also placed on the responsibilities of the master of the craft. For example,in 1639, it was ordered that any such chosen for gild office who had the temerity to refuse to take on that duty would be fined 40 shillings, while any guilty of 'approbrious words' or unseemly behaviour would be 6s. 8d. the poorer for each offence.

So, though we know what was paid for their breakfast in 1543 when 'they went forth', we have no individual records of their return – were they wounded or killed? Did they go missing and remain dead or alive in France? Did they give up capping and enjoy a military life thereafter? Their records like those of most individual citizens of Coventry, are lost, and we shall therefore never know how they finished their days or what their last will and testament revealed.

CHAPTER V

'CEREMONIAL AND DECORUM CONTINUE'

The ritual aspect of gild activities continues to be emphasised throughout the Cappers' records. For example, at their meeting on the 7th June 1680, they ordered that two of the members should 'ride with the Mayor and Alderman of this city at the Great Fairs... [and] they to have for their pains five shillings'.

One hundred years later much the same interests were still dominant in the Cappers' affairs, viz. the Order dated January 1752.

An order for ye Fair

'It is Ordered, Established and Agreed that the Master shall chuse 2 men (that is to say) one to carry the streamer and another to wait on the Follower and they to have 2/6 a piece. Likewise the Boy employed to carry the end of the streamer to have 6d in money & each of the 3 a pair of Gloves, And 3 shillings for ribbons and the Follower a Pair of Gloves and Ribbons.'

Though the mystery plays were over, ceremonial and decorum are still of significance, well into the 19th century. A record of the 1802 meeting notes the intention to attend the public procession on Easter Monday 'in celebration of the Happy Event of the General Peace', five guineas to be subscribed to the costs thereof, specifically for the manufacture of ribbons for cockades and sashes.

'Resolved also that the Master do subscribe Five Guineas from the Estate towards repaying the Expenses thereof – Resolved that Mr Banbury the Father be requested to manufacture or provide ribbons for Cockades and Sashes which shall be worn by each member.'

This was the delusive peace of Amiens – war continued for another dozen years. As late as 1857, a meeting decided that 'if there should be a show at the approaching Fair, five guineas be at the disposal of the Master to be expended on that occasion'. In short, the Cappers liked a show. Ten years later they were spending an equal sum on the annual Godiva procession at 'the Great Fair', though in 1870 they put it to a meeting that attempts to revive the Godiva procession were 'ill-advised'. By 1911 they had relented but only 'upon the strict understanding that all the arrangements for the Company would be made by the Pageant Master and are adequate and appropriate'. In fact, their representation was considered very inadequate and their subsequent subscription towards costs was reduced to show their displeasure. Such hiccups had not disturbed their earlier enthusiasm for processions. In 1897 they had celebrated the Diamond Jubilee of Queen Victoria and in 1902 the accession of her son Edward VII by processing through the city. As late as 1907 the banner (with bearers) was still lent for suitable processions.

Their Order Book records make it clear that the Cappers took these duties seriously, even if there was a theatricality about their interest in fairs and processions. An example is the Order which appeared in 1728 signed by some 20 members.

'The 28th day of Jan AD 1728. It is this day ordered established & agreed upon by the Master, Ancients and

Assistants of the Company & Fellowship of Cappers & Feltmakers in the City of Coventry, That if the said Warden, Ancients or Assistants or any of them shall appear at the said company at the Michaelmas or Choice quarter. Or at ye January or Accompt Quarter, without a Company's Gown, they shall forfeit and pay for the use of the said Company, two shillings and sixpence. [Five years later it was agreed that the fine be no more or less than the shilling.]'

This interest in their dignity of office continued for well over the next hundred years. In 1802 and again in 1814 we find an Order affecting their behaviour at public events where it was made clear that 'Those members who did not have the requisite governmental peace and regularity' could be expelled from the gild.

At this distance of time it is not easy to find evidence for the mood and motivation of the Cappers as they held their official meetings. The physical factors are reasonably clear because for the winter gathering they met in their chapel at two o'clock (which would have been 'dinner time' in those days) partaking of food and drink at their own, or the Master's, expense. In 1745 it was ordered that, at any meeting, they should not spend above 10 shillings to be charged to the Company, but 'shall pay the Overplus out of their own Pockets'. A year later this restrictive ordinance was declared to be 'intirely Void'. And in 1771 it was noted that the Master was allowed three pounds from gild funds to pay for the Company's dinner – that is, for about 18 dinners. Funds were topped up, after 1781, by a one-pound entrance fee for all new members.

Most of the winter meetings were held in the chapel or the room

15ᵗʰ November
1972

Puligny Montrachet 1970

Saumon Fumé

Gammon
and
Broad Beans

Château Lanessan 1953

Canard Sauvage
Petits Pois
Pommes Duchesse

Château Rieussec 1965

Crème Brulée
aux Fruits

Graham 1958

Canapés au Foie
de Volaille

The annual Bean Feasts still
continue, and the Coventry city
archives retain not only the menu
cards but also some of the actual
beans served to Cappers on these
ceremonial occasions.

below it, variously called the Cappers' Room or the Priests' Room. The summer meetings in July or August often took place at the Master's private house, though a variant of this occurred when the Master was Mr Francis William Franklin – he invited his guests to dine at his warehouse. Other meetings were held at inns, as in 1867 when the annual summer dinner or Bean Feast was held at the King's Arms in Kenilworth 'at six o'clock in the afternoon'. The reason for a six o'clock start was that it was customary for the members to play bowls or croquet from 4pm until supper arrived. Later the invitations are marked 'tennis etc'. Before World War II, members usually paid 10 shillings each towards the Bean Feast. Presumably the cost was greater on the few occasions when the summer party travelled farther afield – for instance in 1873 when the Bean Feast was held in London's famous Crystal Palace, recently moved to Sydenham from its original Hyde Park site.

The numbers present at these feasts varied as new members were elected or put forward for election by 'ballot'. At the January meeting in 1776 it was recorded that 'members shall consist of 17 resident members which shall attend the Master at chapel'. Around this time the term frequently used in the Orders was that a citizen had been 'elected a Capper' or 'admitted a freeman of the said Company'. Apparently election was 'balloted for in regular succession as vacancies occur'. In 1837 there are references to the election of 'assistants' to the Company, though no explanation of their status or duties, if any. One problem, common to all such closed societies, was that a citizen might be recommended for membership, but by the time his turn came round his enthusiasm had waned. This was the case with a man named Ford who, in 1798, told the gild that he was 'obliged for the honour done him but had rather decline'. At one meeting in 1803 attendance dropped as low as two.

Light is thrown on how membership affected the finances of the gild by an entry on 5th November 1768 when it was recorded that Sir Richard Glyn, Baronet, be admitted a member. His election was signed as approved by 10 members including Thomas Iliffe. The fees for entry at this time were:

To the Company	10s.6d.
Freeman's Stamp	2s.2d.
Clerk's Fees	2s.6d.
Summoners' Ditto	1s.0d.
Total	16s.2d.

Presumably the 10s.6d. would be, in effect, Sir Richard's annual subscription.

If these were some of the cost of membership, what were the financial benefits, if any? Loans could be acquired, though it is not clear how frequent these were nor whether interest was paid. In January 1779, it was agreed that £20 be granted to young freemen of the city without interest for five years 'upon their Bonde', and the same year a Mr John Owen was loaned £20 for five years upon producing two good securities for the same. Similar loans to other members are recorded, one being in July 1881 to a Joseph Martin who was a watch-springer and -liner.

The gild's income (which will be described more fully later) was at least in part dependent on profit from the rental of property owned by the Company. Towards the end of the 18th century there is record of the grant of a 21-year lease on the Cappers' house in Jordan Well, and earlier there had been notice of a 'rented house and premises known as Hat & Feather at a yearly rent of ten pounds clear of all deductions'. It seems that members of the Company had preferential rights to rent these properties when leases came up for renewal.

Another property which brought in income was the Star & Garter Inn, Bishop Street, at one time leased to Inde Coope and Co Ltd for £45 per annum. Realising its higher value, the Company arranged in 1915 to sell the lease to another brewer for £1500. That deal fell through, but in 1922 a successful sale was agreed at £1640.

The Cappers' inn known as The Hat & Feather stood at the corner of Jordan Well and Much Park Street and was given to the gild by Thomas Oken of Warwick, a well-known benefactor, in the 16th century. Several Cappers were feoffees (probably trustees) of the Oken Estate, including Ralph Browne, Mayor of Coventry in 1573. Another was Hugh Harvey (feoffee of the Estate in 1564 and a sheriff in 1560). A feoffee in the same year was Henry Heath, a third John Heynes, a fourth John Jobberne and a fifth Martin Newnham. Rental income from properties was important not only for the Cappers: Berger describes it as a vital component of the Mercers' budget, becoming a quarter or a half their total income before the mid-1630s, and thereafter two thirds.

From the handwritten pages of the Order and Accounts Books one is able to reconstruct something of the life in medieval Coventry. The following, taken from the Accounts Book of 1573, is typical, though it fails to fill in our knowledge much below the surface. We know from other sources that the capping trade was beginning to fall on hard times. For some years past the city itself, once the wealthiest in the Midlands, had suffered a 'wrecked' economy – with abandoned houses, shabby public buildings and far too many unemployed. Yet there is not much evidence of this in the daily records of the Cappers' gild. They are still able to keep up their chapel, eat their cakes and ale or venison and wine on special days, attend the funerals of their colleagues, process in the fair with their banners, and so on.

Account Book: folio 105 verso [1573]. 'Payments'

(The values are given in medieval Roman numerals – 'x' for 10, 'v' for 5, and 'i' or 'j' for 1 – so that 'ij.s', is read as 2s, 'xviij.d' as 18d, 'vj.s iiij.d' as 6s 4d, and so on.)

Paid to Antony Rydinge for goyng to Lychfeld about ye brief which came from the cappers of London when the queene was at Kylingworth	xij.d
Pd to Mr Oken for a yeares rent	x.s
Spent at Wm Assburns on ye company when we did agree about thychking with Kyng for v.d. a dossen	ij.s
Pd for coales on St Stevens Day	iiij.d

Pd on St Stevens Daye, for Secke
Sugar bread & ale, which was spent in the Chappell   xxij.d

Pd to the Churchwardens for Chappell rent   xij.s
Pd ye .4. of January for bread ale & coles spent in
ye chamber   x.d.

Pd to ye carpenter for mending the pagent house dore   vj.d

Pd to Bawll for his attendaunce ye wholl yere,
& for ye beare   viij.d

Pd on Shof Thursday for coles in ye chamber   ij.d

Pd to Wheeler for Fatching Adlington before Mr Maior   ij.d

Pd to Mych. Tysall for goyng to Wm Russell about
Adlyngtons doynges   vj.d

Pd to Mych. Tysall at ye buriall of Mr Brownell   iiij.d

Pd to ye somner & bearers at ye buryall of
George Harrison   iiij.d

Spent at Mr Waldens on ye Lychfeld men at their
first comyng, concerning Adlington in ye presence
of certayne of ye company   xviij.d

Pd to ye players at ye first rehears   xx.d

Spent ye same mornying at Mr Waldens of certayne
of ye company which came to the rehearse   xviij.d

Spent ye .3. of Aprill at Mr Waldens upon ye
Lychfeld men,at ye ende made betweene them
& Adlington for wyne, sugar & a dyner   vj.s iiij.d

Payd to ye somner & bearers at the buryall of Boydon   iiij.d

Payed to ye players at ye second Rehearse   xviij.d

Pd for making cleane ye chamber   iiij.d

Pd for Rushes that strawed ye Chamber   iiij.d

Pd for harnes, & to ye berers on ye fayr day   xviij.d

Pd to ye Somner, and clarke for ye wholle yere   xij.s

Pd on ye choosinge day for a pottell of clarett wyne,
to drink with the venyson, at the request of certayn
of ye company   x.d

Pd the same daye to ye mynstrells   xviij.d

Pd for making a supplicat'on to my Lord of Leycestr
in parlement, and other letters of request.   viij.d

Pd for engrosynge a copy of the proclamacion which
was dedycated to the queenes matie in parchment   xij.d

Spent at Ric Halls upon Lytler of London   ij.s

At first sight, quotations such as these tell us little about the problems which motivated the gild members. Questions we should like to have answered include: What kind of arrangements did they have to sell their goods through the Mercers, who had the exclusive rights to own shops? Were they suffering competition from foreign industry? Was the smart end of the trade now centred on London? These questions remain unanswered, even though there are indications elsewhere that everything was far from well. For example, the history of the Mercer's company at this period (1550-1680 by Ronald M. Berger) underlines that the rôle of Coventry's city council was primarily to protect trade and its enfranchised citizens.

It is possible that two items which appear towards the end of the above quotation ('for making a supplication to my Lord of Leycester' and 'the proclamacion which was dedicated to the queen's majesty') may have had this very object as their purpose. If so, they will have been precursors of the charter which King James I granted to the city in 1621. Berger describes this as aiming (1) to protect the city's rôle as an essential place of exchange; (2) to limit competition by confining business activity to the chosen few; (3) to allow only those who had been apprenticed locally to trade. He quotes the charter:

> 'No stranger or foreigner [the two words used to describe any 'outsider'] not being a freeman of the said City, shall from henceforth sell, or put to sale, any wares or merchandizes within the said City, otherwise than in gross, and other than victuals and other necessaries for provision and victualling, sold or to be sold within the said City, unless it be during the time of the fairs.... neither shall use or keep open any shop, or use any mystery, manual art, or occupation..... without the special license of the Mayor and Alderman of the said City...'

If the Cappers was a 'closed' gild or craft, no doubt this protected them as it did the Mercers and others, as far as it went, because Berger claims that if such protectionism forced up the retail price of essential commodities 'the corporation [then] abandoned its ideal of upholding exclusive craft privilege'. Its goal of allowing no one but citizens to work and trade in the town was easily set aside. The same lack of rigidity applied to labour – in 1530 when skilled labour was scarce, the council made it legal for all inhabitants, regardless of training, to work as dyers. By the middle of the next century, the city council had, Berger says, lost the ability to enforce ordinances restricting unregulated competition.

One difficulty in interpreting the effect of such restrictions is the need to know to what extent the council and the Leet enforced them with the co-operation of the gild. Or had the gild become – or was it in process of becoming – more of a social brotherhood than an arm of the capping trade? There is some evidence that the town's authorities were doing what they could to uphold the rights of gilds to govern their members for the benefit of their trade. Writing specifically about the Mercers, Berger points to ordinances and bye-laws of 1593 which spoke of 'the Reforminge of Sundrye dysorders and abuses ... to the great disworship [and] discreadite of our whole government in the said felowshipe'. Their object was to create a more powerful central authority. Immediately Coventry's Leet Court , claiming that members of several companies had been disorderly, took steps on 5th May 1593 to support the power of elected gild officials. The Leet stated that if a freeman did not obey craft rules, he could be fined and punished further – with eventual loss of freedom and permanent disenfranchisement.

Berger says that the Mercers' changes of bye-laws were in keeping

Mayors of Coventry

1705	William Byrd	Silkman
1719	Steven Smith	Silkman
1733	Thomas Oldman	Silkman
1743	Thomas Oldman	Silkman
1746	J. Kirkham	Silkman
1753	Thomas Oldman	Silkman
1754	Thomas Oldman	Silkman
1755	John Hewett	Silkman
1758	John Hewett	Silkman
1766	James Soden	Silkman
1773	James Soden	Silkman
1774	James Soden	Silkman
1775	James Soden	Silkman
1780	Thomas Picken	Silkman
1788	Nathaniel Norman	Silkman
1790	James Soden	Silkman
1791	James Soden	Silkman
1797	W. Stanbridge	Silkman
1798	W. Stanbridge	Silkman

This list is taken from the Table of Mayors in St. Mary's Hall

The mayors of Coventry include a number of Cappers, amongst the most prominent being the Owens, notably Edward Owen, believed to have been mayor first in 1635.

with changes in craft structure throughout the country, and quotes other gilds where control was falling into the hands of small groups of wealthy officers, former officers and liverymen. He quotes a history of London gilds which claims that by the mid-seventeenth century the fully developed livery company had become 'strictly oligarchical' (that is, governed by a small group of people, no longer with any pretence of democracy). While there is no specific evidence that this is what was happening to the Cappers, it does appear that there is some indication of a small group of members getting a degree of influence in the brotherhood unconnected with the well-being of the gild as a whole.

For example, there is the strange story of the Owen family, or of a number of people, not all necessarily related, having that name. A Christopher Owen appears first in 1572 and his three sons were apprenticed to the capping trade. The last reference to his name is 1610. Another Christopher Owen, probably born 1604, was a grandson of the original Christopher Owen, and was apprenticed in 1618. He was mayor in 1662, two years after being Sheriff. He was also a St Michael's churchwarden and active on the council until his death in 1670. We are fortunate in possessing a copy of his will, which escaped the bombing of Coventry in 1940 because it was in the archives at Lichfield. This will throws light on the activities of a prominent Capper in relation to his business and social activities.

The Edward Owen (unless there is an overlapping of Christian names) who played a significant part in the story of the Cappers is believed to have been mayor in 1635. The contemporary records show that from 1630-40 the number of Cappers attending gild meetings had become very small indeed. In the year 1637 it fell as low as four members. The Accounts Book for the following year, 1638 (folio 172 verso) shows that the Cappers tried to introduce a Feltmaker into membership, no fee being paid.

[Account for the year 1638, rendered 1638/9 January 20th
'January 28th 1638. Memorandum this day William Barker
Feltmaker is / admitted to be a love brother of this Company
so far as the / Company hath power; and he doth submit himsel
to bee /obedient to all the Orders of the Company / William
Barker.' [Signed - and no fee rendered for admission.]

The above is the very first entry in the Accounts Book under the heading: 'Acct: of Roger Fisher and Abraham Owen late Masters /of the Company and fellowship of Cappers, and felt makers.....'

This is the first time that this new styling appears, referring to feltmaking or Feltmakers, in the Cappers' records.

Earlier it has been suggested that feltmaking brought about the demise of capping as a trade in Coventry. An alternative theory, however, could be that the introduction of feltmaking actually saved the gild from extinction. Here we have one of the Owens introducing a feltmaker to membership in 1638-9 when Edward Owen was mayor. We also need an explanation for an entry in the Order Book *c.*1672 (folio 21). This entry is signed or witnessed by some 125 names and it is so far unexplained why it was that members who were paying their annual fee (quarterage) should on this occasion have done so together in such huge numbers and thus, so to speak, endorsed the entry's statement. The latter reads as follows:

'Mr Edward Owen, sometime Mayor of this City of Coventry; was the first that Brought unto this city; the Art and Mistorie of Feltmaking.'

One can only speculate that this same Edward Owen was proud of having introduced feltmaking to the city and, by implication, of having saved the gild itself from decay. If we assume that he was mayor in 1635 then he is the Owen who five years earlier had, along with two other Cappers, bought their pageant house from the Corporation and in the same year, in company with the gild masters, negotiated the sale of St Thomas's Chapel, adjacent to St Michael's Church, presumably to raise funds. He was said to be an active member of the Council whose portrait survives and now hangs in St Mary's Gild Hall.

An Edward Owen (16??-1705) was Sheriff and then mayor in 1680, although some twenty years later James II had him ejected from his aldermanship for reasons unknown. It is unlikely to have been because he failed to exercise his duties, since it is recorded he had been a justice of the peace and was active on the city council 1679-84 and again after 1688. He was involved with numerous charities and may well have been the most politically active of the Owen family.

By trade he was both a capper and feltmaker.

The fact that Christopher Owen's will of 1670 survives has already been mentioned. A number of the Owen family members left wills. Mostly the proven values by inventory are of only a limited value. The outstanding exception is Christopher Owen's. This man signed his work – an extensive document – on 25th August 1670. Probate was granted on 20th December 1670. The probate documents show him styled as: 'alderman of Coventry' and 'feltmaker'. Probably for financial reasons, he chose to live in the city in a rented house of considerable size. But he himself owned property in Earl Street and in Pinley and Shortley; a dwelling house in Broadgate; a close known as Quarry Close or Priors-quarry; and a barn outside New Gate.

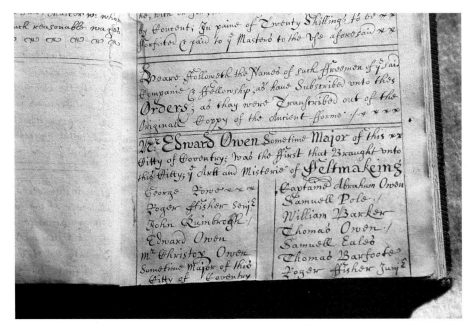

A close-up of the entry for Edward Owen in the Cappers' Order Book which records his claim to be 'the first that Brought unto this city; the Art and Mistorie of Feltmaking'.

The striking document is this man's inventory. There are lists in quantities that would have made even the Mad Hatter envious! At his death he has capital out on loan; and he died owed:

'100 li due from Richard Hopkins esq.

200 li in money in custody of Mr Jn Brownell'.

His total valuation comes to:

'650 li'.

This is no mean amount for those days, probably the equivalent of nearly £50,000 today. To die with substantial loans and debts outstanding was not uncommon in those times. These were cast as 'sperate' or 'desperate' according to expectations. Mercers, for example, left a third of their moveable wealth as loans, though only half of these were likely to be collected.

The Owens were some of the last of the Coventry families to have done some service both as Cappers and as civic officials. Others included Richard Waterfall, Capper and city warden (1672) and Holy Trinity churchwarden (1669); Henry Jephcott, a Capper and Holy Trinity churchwarden (1700); Thomas Smith, joint-master (1726), chamberlain (1729) and sheriff (1744). Curiously, he was described as a hatter and confectioner – presumably in the hatting sense. Benjamin Ward was a Capper and Holy Trinity churchwarden (1732 and 1740).

The medieval Cappers had always had charitable purposes at the heart of their activities, just as other gilds such as the Mercers had looked after their members too. Four main categories of dependent persons received their charitable assistance: the elderly and retired members, widows of members, established craftsmen who were temporarily on hard times and the young without capital. But after the Reformation many craft gilds appear to have re-evaluated their

A page from the Elizabethan
Order Book illustrates how
difficult it is for the modern
reader to follow the calligraphy
without assistance, even though
it may have been quite clear to
the Cappers of the time.

philanthropic activities. Some, certainly, may have increased their charitable giving (particularly after the religious orders were dissolved) but in the main it 'succumbed to the materialism of the Reformation'. Christopher Owen's will of 1670 is evidence of this as far as an individual member is concerned. Agreed, he had substantial sums out on loan, and if the Mercers can be taken as a guide, he will have been charging eight per cent interest from 1617 to 1630, and six per cent thereafter. So far as his gild was concerned it was probably, like Berger's description of the Mercers, still trying to fulfil its charitable responsibilities on a small income and few assets. In comparison, the Cappers were operating on a much-reduced scale.

By the 19th century, if the Order Book is taken as evidence, the Cappers show a tendency to concentrate their activities less on city politics and more on charitable giving to the City and its less well-off members. In 1811 they helped finance the building of a road in the city; in 1816 they are subscribing to the soup establishments (presumably for those worthy poor who had survived the deprivations of Waterloo); in 1835 it is repairs to the organ in St Michael's; in 1850 towards the building of a hospital; in 1875 to the cost of the city's steam fire engine. Alas, no details of these various donations are given, for certainly some must have told a story. One example is the 1905 donation to The Friendless Girls' Association. Another comes as late as 1933 – three guineas to the Oil Acid Society. More significant were the contributions made to the new Coventry Cathedral and to Warwick University about which more is said on p. 135.

Incidentally this Order Book, so valuable today, probably appears in the Accounts Book for 1671 as follows:

Payd for A paper book to enter Orders in   1s.4d.

CHAPTER VI

'THE INDUSTRIAL REVOLUTION'

In the days when wool had reigned supreme, Coventry had claimed to be the industrial and commercial centre of the Midlands, switching to silk ribbon with the decline of woollen manufacturing. But once the new age of coal and iron became pre-eminent, the city – which had coal but no iron – gradually lost ground to Birmingham and the Black Country, which had both. Before the beginning of the 19th century Coventry ceased to be a great provincial capital.

It might be thought that the coming of the railways would have put new life into the communications system on which Coventry depended for its status, but the truth is that the city had very little use for the iron roads. Coal was delivered by canal, and its own deliveries of ribbon were easily moved around by coach and horses.

The first thing that must have struck the visitor in 1830 was that the city was now small, dirty and overcrowded. Though it was surrounded by pastures and parkland – the latter belonging to the aristocracy – this land could not be built on until it was enclosed by Act of Parliament, and no such Act was forthcoming. The city itself retained many fine 16th- and 17th-century half-timbered houses and early Georgian brick ones (like those round the cathedral today) but during the 18th century they were 'in-filled' by speculators, whose prime target was to build on the gardens of the earlier, more spacious, abodes.

A map of the area round Much Park Street, drawn in 1851 after the property developers had got at it, indicates that about 1000 people co-existed in an area about 600 ft long and 360 ft wide. This was typical of the crowded courts and yards where the workers lived with too little air, bad water from a well which served perhaps a dozen families, and cesspits but no main sewer. There was no paving or lighting here and probably no direct access to a road.

The only people who could have changed this state of affairs – had they so wished – were the freemen of the city. Young people could gain this distinction by serving a registered apprenticeship to a trade for seven years; it didn't matter which trade it was, though most were weavers or watchmakers. This freedom, won by apprenticed servitude, brought with it the reward of the franchise – for men only of course. Before the Reform Act of 1832 this was the only qualification for voting for one's Member of Parliament.

For the 30-odd years after the 1832 Reform Act, the Coventry freemen dutifully returned Liberal or Radical members to Parliament. However their hold over the corporation itself was not equally powerful. The city was run by a Grand Council of about 30 members which met annually to elect the officers of the Leet. It was the latter – the mayor, the aldermen and the town clerk – who held power in their hands. And they were, by modern standards, corrupt. Indeed, many would forego a salary in return for the benefits of the influence that went with office. They wielded patronage, issued city contracts and even sat on the Bench, thus influencing the local police and the military, exercising the control previously in the hands of the gilds.

It was not impossible for a manufacturer to acquire status by becoming a member of the Coventry corporation – the city's ruling body – and in *Middlemarch* George Eliot says that Mr Vincy the ribbon-maker had aspirations to be made mayor. He had plenty of cash which he spent on taking his friends coursing, and on the fine cellar from which he produced bottles to entertain his more influential colleagues. But the majority of Corporation members had been professional men – bankers (like Eliot's Mr Bulstrode), lawyers and even landed aristocracy – that is, they held the majority until the 1830s. Once the Radicals came to

A silk ribbon sample book for the years 1805-10, when Coventry was supreme in this fashion industry. The surviving brand-name today is Cash's.

power in 1832, changes were made which fundamentally improved the city. Building land became available, and, within a generation, there were fresh water supplies. By 1851, nearly half the city's 8000 houses were supplied with clear water from a mains supply. A sewage system followed, then building regulations. Indeed, by the mid-1850s, Coventry was well on the way to becoming a model city and its death rate began to fall.

Over the previous 100 years or so cloth had been replaced as the dominant industry by silk ribbon manufacture, and this was the birth of manufacturing industry here as we know it today. According to Daniel Defoe, the first ribbons made in Coventry were black, but about the turn of the century – certainly before 1710 – a Mr Bird

Spinning wheels and looms remained in use in Coventry's homes, like that rented by this weaver couple, the Harrisons, in 1896. Working conditions are described as 'a disgrace'.

introduced an expansion of ribbon manufacture to the city, using French workmen from Lyons and Tours. Soon there were about 13,000 looms supporting 30,000 silk workers, while cloth itself suffered from what was described as 'a very fatal damp'. Inevitably, as the Industrial Revolution took hold, silk-ribbon weaving also caught a cold, because ribbons made in Coventry met competition with French or Swiss production, after being protected for well over 50 years by the prohibition of imports. Now, the growing belief in Free Trade led to the substitution of a protective tariff; in 1830 this was 25 per cent. The result was that the European manufacturers supplied the British upper-class trade while Coventry supplied the lower classes. As for plain ribbons, Coventry, Derby, Leek and Congleton supplied virtually the whole of the UK.

Silk was imported, and 'thrown' before being sent on to the

Coventry weavers in the hank. They then dyed and wove it before sending it on to distributors. None of them dealt with the retailers direct. A pool of casual labour was employed to deal with seasonal variations or sudden demands from the fashion trade, though by the 1830s, to provide better supervision, there was already a move towards a factory system, where the weavers worked regular hours. The labour was somewhat specialised and it was some time before there was any ambitious move towards mechanisation. While there had been machinery such as looms since the turn of the century, it was not until 1831 that the first steam factory was built in Coventry. This unpopular introduction led to a workers' riot, and for the next six years no attempt was made to introduce steam-driven machinery to the city again.

A survey of 1838 showed that while there were 7000 single hand looms in the surrounding countryside, there were only 130 in the city itself, where several thousand much bigger machines were employed. Three quarters of the country weavers were said to be women or children. The children went to work when they were between eight and ten years old. No child earned more than one shilling and sixpence a week, and this miserable wage was paid to its parents. Children were expected to work from 7am to 8pm, though they had Sunday and Monday off. Prior to working they had probably attended a dame or charity school for a couple of years. It was, to coin a phrase, weaving from cradle to grave and, while there is no direct evidence to support it, the attitude of Coventry citizens from the Middle Ages right through to the end of the 19th century may well have been that they were entitled to a job in the wool trade, or in some business connected with it.

One of the powers which the Leet had allocated to itself was employment regulation, in the sense that if a man could work, he came under strict conditions which virtually forced him to take up an apprenticeship followed by fellowship of a craft union, carrying with it freedom of the city. By this means the flow of immigrants was controlled. Thus, despite the decline in the cloth trade over the 16th and 17th centuries, the preponderance of those who worked in Coventry in the 18th century still made a living in it, one way or another. A minority threw in their hand, and many relied for a living on herds of cattle which they kept on the common land.

Two major changes were made in apprenticeship practice at this time. One was that from 1668 masters of gilds had to report to the mayor the names of their apprentices, who in turn had to swear the oath of a freeman before the mayor when their term was completed. Their names were then enrolled in the 'sword-bearers' book'. The other change was the foundation of charities connected with apprentices – charities which took the form in the Cappers' case of enabling them to borrow money at low or non-existent terms of interest.

Such charitable arrangements must have encouraged the 'cradle to the grave' mentality, and this, coupled with the fact that related businesses came to Coventry to fill the gap previously held by the wool-cloth industry, meant that the weavers' trade continued to be popular. In 1707 it was said that the city enjoyed 'a good inland trade by the cloth here vended' and the same might have been said for the next 150 years, largely thanks to the growth of silk-weaving and the silk ribbons trade.

A few figures illustrate the continued popularity of the weavers' trade in Coventry in the 17th and 18th centuries. Of the 70 'masters' admitted to freedom of the city in 1640, over 60 were engaged in various branches of the cloth trade. A hundred years later, there were about the same number of admissions, about half being silk weavers. In 1734, the number of admissions shot up to 571, of whom 372 were weavers. These men performed their civic duties – the list of constables appointed in the hundred years from 1733 contained a majority of weavers. They were organised,

From the 1830s and '40s, fashionable dresses like this were extensively embellished with silk ribbon, covering the person literally from head to foot.

too, the silk weavers forming a fellowship in 1627 and the worsted weavers splitting off to form another in 1703.

Wages in the city were paid by the piece, and there was a 'List' of prices so that, effectively, wages control was in operation – though some of the less scrupulous employers ignored this 'List'. When work was scarce, the unemployed weaver might go 'on the parish', though if he were a freeman he might be entitled to benefit from some of the charitable funds established by the city, or by his gild. The richer citizens also provided charity in kind by gifts to the poorer, probably taking the form of bread, potatoes and some tea supplemented by scraps of bacon or milk.

Prest, writing about this period, says that country working life was a disgrace. Inside the cottages, scattered round the weaver, there might be a stool, an old table and a chair, the bed, made of straw if the family was 'well off', and a bedstead made of bricks. George

Ribbon contrived to be a feature of women's dress fashion well into the Victorian age, and clothes like this dress were no doubt the admiration of George Eliot's wealthier heroines.

Eliot describes the weaver as 'a pale, sickly looking man or woman pressing a narrow chest against a board, and doing a sort of treadmill work with legs and arms'. The girls were pregnant before they married at sixteen or seventeen, and bastardy was common. There were few large houses where they could go into domestic service, and, in any case, the men preferred to marry weavers because they brought a wage with them.

The story was different in the agricultural area south of the city, according to Prest, who notes that many good cottages were available there at low rents, so one saw tidy gardens and well-clothed children. The city centre too, was better, with the tone set by freemen and journeymen. The weaver could find houses which might be rented for a mere £8-10 a year. Entered from the back through the scullery, there was a comfortable kitchen with its range. From there, a staircase led upstairs to the big room at the back used as a workshop, and to the two bedrooms in the front. The better-off had three-storey houses, with the top floor given over to the looms. To keep the house itself free of the noise of the weaving, rags were stuffed between floor and ceiling for insulation.

Silk-weaving was not always a healthy occupation, because the windows had to be kept closed, as the weaver worked without a fire which would have smoked and damaged the ribbon. He was cramped, too, with his chest pressed against the loom while he worked. Prest believes the workers suffered mainly from stress and particularly from fear of unemployment. There was, however, the solace of country life not far away.

This, then, was the background to the structure of mid-19th-century life in the Coventry area, glued together by the 'List' of prices and wages. It had begun before 1700 and continued for over 150 years. Its success held for about 30 years after the Reform Bill, until, in 1860, the whole system collapsed. This was a period during which the population of the city approximately doubled, and it was also a period in which the watchmaking industry, introduced at

the beginning of the century, continued to expand. By 1851 there were over 2000 employed in this trade. Women did not participate, as a watchmaking husband could, alone, earn as much as a couple could in the weaving business. What is more, it was a 'cottage industry' of small workshops, unlike weaving which was progressively being centred on the factory.

Elaborate watches were the speciality of Coventry makers after their introduction at the beginning of the 19th century. By 1851 there were over 2000 people, mostly men, employed in this trade.

As a result, the class of apprentice freeman weavers could not compete with factory-organised labour, so they

This Jacquard loom, from the 1820s, is a replica in the Herbert Museum in Coventry. The new textile factories were steam-driven, threatening the small cottage weavers with their hand machines.

gradually forsook ribbon-making for the watch business – anyway, the potential freeman much preferred working at home. Curiously, as the journeyman weavers fell on hard times, there were already signs that the watchmakers too would decline. More of this later.

Returning to the period 1840-60, this was marked by the establishment of new textile factories, particularly those that were steam-driven. Any factory constructed after 1850 in Coventry would have been a steam factory, built under licence to local board of health designs. Throughout the 1850s, the journeymen tried to compete by building 'cottage factories' which had steam engines at the ends of their rows of weaver's houses. These became a serious threat to the big factories. Indeed in 1859 there were 15 large factories with 1250 power looms versus 300 of the small cottage factories with anything up to six looms each. The two systems were thus competing neck and neck in terms of the number of looms. For a brief period, the cottage system triumphed and no big factories were built between 1858 and 1860.

Something is known about the way the cottage factories worked because one of their skilled employees, William Andrews, kept a diary. He had finished his apprenticeship in 1855 and became a designer at £100 p.a. with the firm of John & Joseph Cash (the name survives today in Cash's Nametapes). They were enlightened employers, since the brothers were benevolent Quaker capitalists. They sent Andrews to Paris to acquire the finishing touches to his skills, and, back in London, they kept him in the social scene by buying him a ticket to see the actor Kean in Shakespeare's *Richard II*, probably at Drury Lane. He enjoyed proper holidays (not like the general run of workers who only had Christmas, Good Friday and Easter off) and he was given a company house in the complex Cash's had built at Cash's Lane, Kingsfield. From there he managed the cottage weaving business which occupied 100 families.

Prest says that the Kingsfield cottages still stand as 'a monument that ought to be preserved to a lost industrial system and a number of forgotten ideals'. One of the Cash brothers also formed The Coventry Labourers' and Artisans' Friendly Society, its object being to supply working men with gardens where they could grow food – in its heyday it had 400 such gardens. These were in effect allotments, where poorer people could provide themselves with food for free, and since it supplied members also with goods like coal and flour it became in time the first Coventry co-operative society. The Cashs had plans to build 300 cottages round a steam engine but alas, when the ribbon trade collapsed in 1860, the Friendly Society collapsed with it.

The issue was simple: every manufacturer who installed new

machinery must pay the same 'List' price 'per piece' as that which the cottage weavers received for work on their own older looms. 'Back to the 'List' prices' was the cry. In an attempt to force this through, the two sides of the labour force combined to use the strike weapon to obtain their ends. The struggle began on 4th September 1858, but the big manufacturers responded by declaring war in the form of a lock-out. For a time they were defeated, and, as noted above, no weaving factories were built after 1857. Prest makes the point that 'if the masters who installed expensive machinery, and paid the highest weekly wages in town, were to be forced to pay the weavers the same price per piece that they paid before there was any [factory] machinery at all, then mechanisation must stop'. Both sides became bitter and remained so through 1859.

Early in 1860 the rumour reached Coventry that the government was negotiating a 'Free Trade' commercial treaty with France that would lead to a reduction in the 15 per cent tariff on foreign ribbons. On 10th February, Gladstone told the House of Commons that the duty was to be lifted *in toto*. A London newspaper wrote that Coventry:

> 'is probably in a less satisfactory condition than any other
> manufacturing district in England..... Little enterprise is
> manifested by the master manufacturer, and still less by
> the operator weaver..... They seem to jog on in the old style
> in which their grandfathers pursued their trade, and to
> trust to foreign skill to provide them with new ideas.'

Worse was to befall this unambitious industry. The French continued to tax British imports of ribbons; the American ribbon manufacturers began to export aggressively; the fashion industry switched from ribbons to feathers; the silkworms caught a disease;

then the Coventry workers cut their own throats by developing a full-blown labour dispute. Trade steadily declined. Finally, the manufacturing bosses decided in July 1860 to abandon the 'List'. A strike of great bitterness followed when the number of people out of work probably reached 30,000.

Meanwhile, the weavers of St Etienne in France and Basle in Switzerland worked overtime to supply the British market with ribbons. By 1865 more than half the British manufacturers had been made bankrupt. The weavers sold their furniture and pawned their Sunday clothes – so there was little to be gained by hounding more of them into bankruptcy. Trade failed to recover and the out-of-work weavers began to leave town *en masse*. Census returns for the decade after 1861 showed the Coventry population decreased from 41,546 to 39,991 – this in a region where the population had been increasing all through the 19th century. In the same period, Leamington's population went up by 3,508, Leicester's by 27,164 and Birmingham's third of a million by a massive 47,711.

Some of the emigrants went far afield; for instance the diarist William Andrews worked in France and Switzerland for 18 months in all, returning to Cash's as a designer at £100 a year – the same salary he had started with, at the same firm, six years earlier. He noted on his return, too, that the cottage factory at Kingsfield had failed. He was later to be its manager once again.

Prest points out that this industrial revolution did not occur either as a sole result of the invention of the steam engine or the resultant revolution in transport. Its key factor was the substitution of competition for the medieval regulators which had previously controlled the production and distribution of wealth – in other words the 'List'.

Another factor must have been the surge of other industrial

development in the city, notably watchmaking, and, deriving from it, the manufacture of the cycle and then the motor car.

A local trade in watchmaking had began towards the end of the 17th century and a member of the trade became sheriff in 1685. Another was mayor in 1727, 1745 and 1753. Unfortunately the council, at a time of economic retrenchment, ceased in 1706 to pay the watchmaker for the care of the city's clocks, a severe financial blow. Little is heard of the business thereafter until about 1750, when the first of the Rotherams, John Bottrill, began to develop the craft again. Another, Samuel Vale, was also prominent, becoming four times mayor. An indication of the status of the business was that in the next 100 years many watchmakers became constables.

By 1830 there were at least 53 watchmakers in the county directory, 142 in 1850, six of which still survived into the 1930s. The period of greatest development was between 1830 and 1850. Unlike the ribbon trade, watchmaking was a craft skill which could not, in those days, be threatened by machines, and was not amenable to any form of mass production. No factories competed with the individual maker's shops, which were mainly in the Spon End and Chapel Fields areas. The attractions of such a trade caught on and while in the 1830s nearly half the apprentices in Coventry were weavers, by the 1850s only 20 per cent joined this traditional business, while over half were going into watchmaking. By 1851 it is estimated that some 2000 were employed in watchmaking, and trade was good with both satisfactory profits and wages. For a brief period, Coventry was Britain's biggest maker of watches, exporting them to all parts of the Empire. Inevitably excessive competition from home and abroad led to the production of cheaper watches and by 1858 there was a depression. The most serious decline was after 1890.

ROTHERHAM & SONS,

| INTERCHANGEABLE CASES. EXTRA DURABLE AND DUST PROOF. | Coventry and London, | INTERCHANGEABLE MATERIAL FOR REPAIRS. |

WATCH MANUFACTURERS,

JUROR: INVENTIONS EXHIBITION, LONDON, 1885.

PARIS 1889

GOLD MEDALS.

MELBOURNE 1888

LONDON 1851

PRIZE MEDALS.

LONDON 1862

CHRONOGRAPHS, REPEATERS, AND ADJUSTED WATCHES IN EVERY VARIETY.

AL RAD OF ENGLISH LEVER WATCHES, KEYLESS AND NON-KEYLESS.

Messrs. ROTHERHAM & SONS obtained the Highest Record for Complicated Watches at the Kew Observatory Trials for the years 1890 and 1891.

Price Lists of Watches, and Illustrated Catalogue of Interchangeable Material for "Rotherham" Watches, supplied to the Trade upon application.

Rotherham & Sons of Spon Street survived and by the end of the century they were employing 400-500 men making 100 watches a day. But by 1935 the number of firms had declined so sharply that only a handful remained. In 1945, only two were left, both of them in their original premises, one being Rotherham, which celebrated its bi-centenary in 1950, the other Alexander & Son which celebrated its in 1960. Excessive competition from abroad has, of course, finally killed off this once notable city industry. Between 1727 and 1832 there had been 12 Coventry mayors proud to describe themselves at watchmakers. After that date none did so.

By 1830 there were at least 53 watchmakers in the county directory, the most prominent being the Rotherham family, and for a brief period Coventry was Britain's biggest maker of watches, exporting them to all parts of what was called the British Empire. Rotherham's survived until after 1950.

Compare the clarity of this handwriting from the 1719 Accounts Book with that of earlier Cappers from the Elizabethan times, reproduced on page 93.

But the residue of watchmaking skills in the city in the mid-19th century brought about yet another change of direction which would have far-reaching results. This was the formation of the Coventry Sewing Machine Company. Problems of one kind and another dogged the firm and left business slack at the end of the 1860s. In 1867 the company's enterprising Paris agent, a Rowley B. Turner, persuaded his bosses to diversify and accept an order for 400 'boneshaker' cycles for sale in France, where the bicycle had been developed. Thus came about the establishment of Coventry as a centre, first of the British cycle trade, and later of the motor industry.

Coventry was well equipped to handle the nascent cycle industry. Little capital was needed and manufacture was often in small 'shop' premises which had been a tradition in Coventry since the days of the Cappers' woollen business. It also remained a good centre to receive components from nearby industry in Birmingham, the Black Country, Sheffield, Walsall, Redditch and so on. It is said that bicycle-making saved Coventry from terminal decline after the slow collapse of the ribbon industry.

What part did the Cappers and other Coventry medieval gilds play in this period, now universally termed a 'revolution'? In his classic book on the Industrial Revolution in Coventry, Prest makes no mention of them, though he has plenty to say about weavers. We know that prominent members of the traditional industries like the Cashs remained members of the gild, but they were now in the minority. Other members were increasingly drawn from the new industries like watchmaking and transport. The next chapter brings the story of the gild up to the present day, with members like Rotherams prominent in the brotherhood. The relationship between gild and government had changed fundamentally. In Henry VIII's time, no gild could

Rotherham's specialised in elaborate clocks as well as watches, and were rewarded for their skills by becoming not only the largest such concern but also the longest survivor. Family members were also prominent Cappers.

execute an ordinance until it had been approved by the city Leet or central government; as time went on, the power of the gilds deteriorated. They became in the words of the historian Prest, 'little more than auxiliary weapons of the town oligarchy'. They were pretty blunt weapons at that.

CHAPTER VII

'IN SILENCE LET US REMEMBER COMMUNITY'

(THE BISHOP OF COVENTRY DEDICATING THE NEW CAPPERS' ROOM IN 1957)

The delicate web which was woven between the watchmaking industry of the late 19th century – Coventry watches were never intended for the mass market – and the sewing machine industry which in turn bred the cycle industry, cannot be disentangled cleanly. But the men who were involved in these various industries often had much in common, including membership of the Cappers. The Rotherham family, for example, were prominent in the gild, though they had long ago given up any concern with watchmaking, and some of them had gone in to the legal profession.

Other names which recurred were the Jaggers, the Iliffes, the Twists, the Cashs and the Browetts, all families said to hold a leadership position in the city hierarchy.

The Rotherhams and Twists had always been Anglican, while the Cashs and Browetts were long-serving Quakers. By the early 20th century, says the historian Richardson, 'the older men gave a very real social leadership to the city' through their work in the charities and through the surviving six gilds, the Cappers being one. Their young sons were sent to public schools, often Rugby (they had introduced its game to the city as early as 1873). At school they trained in the Officers' Training Corps (OTC) and would go on to join the Territorials, from which it was an easy step to a commission in the Royal Warwickshire Regiment. A quarter of all the commissioned officers gave their lives in World War I, a form of charitable giving which their fathers had not had to face, though those Cappers whose sons had enlisted in the war had a terrible price to pay. A brass tablet records the facts. It was affixed to the south wall of the Chapel of St Thomas or the Cappers' Chapel sometime in the 1920s when the chapel was refloored and generally restored. It bears the following names. An asterisk indicates that the officer was killed in action, and is seen to be applied to five out of the 11 sons of Cappers listed.

MEMBERS:
William Fitzthomas Wyley, Col. 7th [Royal Warwickshire Regiment]
Ewan Rotherham, Captain 7th [R. War. Regt]

SONS OF CAPPERS:
*Arnold L. T. Browett, Captain 7th [R. War. Regt]
*Lionel G. Graham, Captain 7th [R. War. Regt]
*Noel F. Graham, Captain 11th [R. War. Regt]
Norris L. Graham, Lieut. R.F.C. [Royal Flying Corps]
Colin C. Graham, Flight Lieut. R.A.F. [Royal Air Force]
A. H. Jagger, Captain 7th [R. War. Regt]
*O. R. O. Jagger, Midshipman R.N. [Royal Navy]
John H. Lorrimer, Lieut. R.A.F.
Ernest Twist, Lieut.-Col. 13th Hussars
Wilfrid Twist, Captain Durham L.I. [Light Infantry]
*W. R. F. Wyley, Lieut. R.F.A. [Royal Field Artillery]

The Victorian age in England is often thought of as the peak period of charitable good works and insofar as this is true, Coventry men followed the trend. Lord Leigh, for example, had established the Leigh Mills in the 1860s to alleviate distress caused by the collapse of the ribbon industry. Later, when the watchmaking industry also declined, and continued to do so into the 20th century under pressure from Swiss competition, the Coventry men involved in it reacted with characteristic Victorian fortitude. One of the most prominent, a member of the Newsome family, attended his office in the Butts every evening until shortly before his death in 1947, though he had not sold a watch since 1904.

Another Newsome, Samuel Theo, who died in 1930, had had the prescience to put his money into the theatre, becoming managing director of the Coventry Hippodrome in 1907. He was followed in this venture by his son, also Samuel, who was master of the Cappers gild in 1948-9 and 1965-6.

It has already been noted that the watch-making skills in the city led to the formation of the Coventry Sewing Machine Company, which in turn diversified into cycles. Apart from the Riley brothers, most of the leaders of this growing cycle industry were immigrants. An example was James Starley, born to a gardener from the East End of London, who came to Coventry in 1872 at the invitation of his uncle, an inventor with an office in Coventry. The uncle started a cycle business which Starley controlled until it was sold to another firm. In 1885 he produced the 'Rover' bicycle, the first popular make. The name would live on to the Millennium as a valuable brand in the new automotive industry.

Starley was not a Capper, but another Coventry citizen who benefited from the growth of the cycle industry would become one.

He was a member of the Iliffe family. William Iliffe had kept a stationer's shop at the corner of Smithford Street and Vicar Lane, where he also ran a growing jobbing printing business. His son William Issac was apprenticed to the ribbon trade, but after its 1860 crash he returned to his father's business. In 1878 he began to publish *The Cyclist* in collaboration with the pioneer Henry Sturmey, and shortly afterwards recruited Alfred Harmsworth, later Lord Northcliffe, to edit *Bicycling News*. In 1895 he launched *The Autocar*. The Iliffes also made a lasting imprint on regional newspapers including the *Midland Daily Telegraph* in 1892 (now the Coventry Evening Telegraph). Their growth in circulation was necessary to meet the demand of the city's burgeoning population.

This expanding population also required more homes, and these were provided by the great men of the city – many of them Cappers. W. I. Iliffe was much concerned with the expansion of the Cheylesmore development, Lord Leigh with Stoneleigh. At the millenium, the latter estate has once more come to residential use in the hands of Kit Martin.

As in all areas of urban growth, there was a tendency for the social leaders to congregate their homes in an exclusive neighbourhood – in this case the district of Coundon Green. The most imposing mansion built there was that of William Hillman, whose social 'set' there at one time or another included the Rotherhams, Cashs, Jaggers, Iliffes, Twists and Browetts. The last two of these families had stood for more than a generation as the twin pillars of the Coventry legal profession. They managed to combine their legal work with

Opposite: The Rover safety bicycle (top) was made in the 1880s in Coventry, masterminded, like most other cycles, by men who were immigrants to the city. One of these was James Starley, and the brand name he gave to his machine has lived on. By the 1890s (below) the most sophisticated and expensive bicycles had pneumatic tyres.

a series of public offices, such as clerks to the magistrates, which they held on a part-time basis. Their names crop up, too, in the pages of the Cappers' Accounts Book. After his father's death, Walter Browett continued the legal practice and was master in 1928-9, and his son Charles Browett was master in 1940-1, one of the most difficult years for the gild as well as the city. Nevertheless Browett is said to have enjoyed acting as host at gild dinners. These always included a dish to illustrate the fact that these had once been gatherings of poor people – bacon and beans in the case of the Cappers (the Weavers had tripe and onions). Other Cappers with legal connections were the Rotherhams, whose number included Richard, a noted solicitor at the turn of the century. Another lawyer of distinction was Malcolm Pridmore (1869-1945), member of an old city family, who served on the council from 1905 to 1934 and is described as philanthropist who supported new housing for the growing city. Another Pridmore, Alexander, was master of the Cappers in 1938-9.

Charles Browett was succeeded as master by his legal partner and son-in-law Arthur Jagger (1895-1962), another member of a family well established in Coundon Green. His wife is listed by the historian Richardson as among the 'leaders of the local community' along with that other lawyer Harold Twist, master in 1935-6.

There was no direct connection, of course, between the Cappers and the growing Coventry motor industry, but it was almost impossible to avoid involvement of some kind in the heady half-century of motor car development. Arthur Jagger's father, for instance, had been invited by his neighbour in Coundon Green to become chairman of the Singer Motor Company, a firm much respected amongst the hundreds of automotive concerns which had sprung up all over the city. George Singer, its founder, had migrated to Coventry to join Stanley's

ALFRED HERBERT LTD., COVENTRY, ENGLAND.

cycle concern in the 1860s, and the Singer name and its prosperous record pushed its owner up the social ladder – he became mayor in 1891-3. Arthur Jagger, whose family had at one time owned a silk mill, prospered in his turn and earned a position in the city based on the Singer connection.

This universal grinding machine from the 1920s' catalogue typifies the new machine tool industry built up in the city by Alfred Herbert, later a Capper and a knight.

Richardson says: 'it is impossible to exaggerate the immense self-confidence with which the pre-1914 young men working in Coventry approached the making of motor cars.... No one can be quite certain he has a complete list of the [types] manufactured in those early days', when the cycle men were transforming their two- and three-wheelers into motor carriages. From about 22 motor cycle firms in 1905 there must have been 50 car companies by the end of World War I. Everyone joined in, even the grand families like the Leighs, whose baronetcy had been established in 1839. Lord Leigh allowed Siddeley to name one of his cars after the Leigh estate at Stoneleigh. Another Capper, William I. Iliffe, though he did not go in to manufacture, became, as has been noted, a partner with the successful engineer Henry Sturmey in *The Cyclist* newspaper, which was later followed by *The Autocar*.

All this activity transformed Coventry into a different kind of city. The 1901 census shows a population of about 70,000. This is not a large figure by today's standards, but during the first half of the 20th century Coventry's population increased, mainly by immigration and the boom time of two wars, to something like five times the 1901 figure.

A pattern of engineering accessory firms clustering around the big manufacturers had already been established earlier by the cycle industry, and this pattern continued – indeed encouraged – the advance towards a motor industry. Not the least of these was of course the new machine tool industry, established largely by the enterprise of Sir Alfred Herbert. He was born into a comfortable middle-class family founded by his father, a building contractor who became a farmer and sent his son Alfred to private school. The young man later bought a partnership in a machine tool company which expanded so successfully that when war broke out in 1914 he had some 2000 employees in the largest such company in the country. It was not unhelpful that his elder brother William became Hillman's partner in his huge cycle business, which had moved into car production in 1905.

Another Capper heavily involved in the machine tool industry was Sir Stanley Harley, who took over the running of the Coventry Gauge & Tool from its founder, his father, Sir Harry. Sir Stanley, a leading Anglican himself, introduced one of the first industrial chaplains to his works. He was master of the Cappers in 1962/3.

Hillman was, of course, a prominent Capper with an imposing house and six daughters, several of whom married, so to speak, in to the motor industry. The bridegrooms included such prestigious names as Louis Coatalen, the French designer who eventually joined Sunbeam, Sir John Black, later to run the Standard company, and Spencer Wilks, who left Hillman (where he had been managing director) when Rootes took it over in 1928. He and his brother then revived the fortunes of Rover.

Another prominent Capper was, curiously, an American, though he obtained British citizenship well before his election as master in 1926-7 and again in 1939-40. This was Percy Martin (1871-1958). He was recruited by Daimler's in the early 1900s to replace James Critchley, who had left to join the Brush electrical firm. Daimler had a somewhat chequered history and had relied largely for their promotion on royal patronage – their cars were a favourite of Edward VII. Though an American, Martin did more to make Daimler's available to Englishmen than their royal fan. He became managing director in 1906 and was getting the Daimler show on the road when World War I broke out. His ability was

recognised by Sir James Weir, brought in by the government to speed up aircraft supplies, who appointed Martin to ginger up the aero-engine industry, largely

Another Capper, the American Percy Martin, was recruited by Daimler in the early 1900s and became managing director of the firm in 1906.

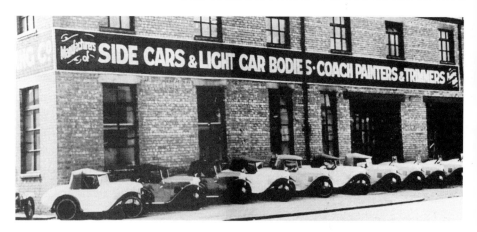

The Capper William Lyons was determined to establish his sidecar company in Coventry, where the automotive industry was so busy that it 'just didn't notice the Depression'.

Coventry-based. After the war he returned to Daimler, now joined with BSA, but in 1933 he retired to his farm at Kenilworth, where he devoted himself to rearing pedigree Guernsey cattle.

After World War I, from which the motor industry had profited considerably, there were problems which suggested that Coventry would suffer heavily from the social stresses of the peace. In early 1921 the proportion of unemployed engineering workers in the West Midlands reached 22 per cent of the total and less than six months later it had climbed to its peak of 33 per cent. However by the year end, employment had stabilised, due to the popularity of the motor car and the establishment of new mechanical engineering industries such as machine tools, telephones and synthetic fibres. Small enterprises were to enjoy success once they were established in the city – for example William Lyons was determined that his Swallow Sidecar Company should be established in Coventry in the 1920s where they were so busy that, in the words of one employee, they 'just didn't notice the Depression'. Lyons became a Capper in 1950 and took an active interest in its affairs.

As far as industry overall was concerned, prosperity seemed assured when rearmament proper began in 1936 with a programme presented by the government to a meeting of West Midland motor manufacturers (Nuffield was a notable absentee by his own choice). Thus began the Shadow Factory Scheme under which the motor men took on the building of aircraft and their engines. However, the scheme got off to a slow start, and in the spring of 1940 there were still over one million unemployed in the country at large.

The story of Coventry's virtual destruction in that first year of World War II is well-known. The night of 14th November was, in the words of the historian Angus Calder, 'the beginning of a new phase' of warfare. It was the first city to be attacked using a new method of sending beams from two radio stations on the Continent. The Germans first fired the medieval centre and then launched a 10-hour attack on the city generally. One third of its housing was made uninhabitable, and the transport system wrecked – buses and trains destroyed. Some 554 people were killed and more than that seriously wounded. Further raids were to follow. Historians claim that this raid was a precedent for the even more terrible attacks later made on Dresden and Hiroshima, and a new word was invented (Coventration) to describe the destruction of a city's civilian population.

Somehow, Coventry recovered to become a booming and vital centre of British war production. In London there was an exodus from the bombed areas and the city generally, but workers continued to arrive in Coventry. According to the government's Production Efficiency Board the result was not what those at the centre of planning would have wished – there was a 'lack of manpower discipline which management was aware of but felt powerless to remedy'.

Coventry, with its labour problems, had now become a centre of one of the biggest national automotive industries in the world. The city fathers saw the dangers of such concentration – by the 1950s, vehicles and mechanical engineering represented nearly two thirds of the total employed – but their attempts to introduce diversification, says Richardson, met with 'very little success'. It might be said that the Cappers, too, had not really prepared the ground for expansion during the late Victorian and Edwardian years. In the half-century to 1920 there were only 24 new members elected, slightly less than one every two years.

For the gild, a particular tragedy of World War II was the destruction of their room and chapel in the first German raid on the city. Little could be done by way of repair during the war itself, and fortunately their invaluable records – the Order Book and the Accounts Book – had been safely stowed away. The decision to rebuild the Cathedral had been taken as early as 1942.

The gild put in a claim for war damage to their property in 1943. The equipment in the chapel and the Cappers' Room had been assessed by the district valuer as worth £100, excluding the structural damage to roof and stained-glass window. The former was agreed, the latter re-submitted to the War Damage Commission. A request to have accommodation in the 'new' cathedral was put forward to the cathedral authorities, and in the event a room to replace the old one was agreed.

By 1955, building work on the 'new' cathedral to the design of the architect Sir Basil Spence was well ahead. The choice of Spence was the responsibility of a committee made up of several leading Cappers, who were also notable benefactors to the costs of the new cathedral. The Cappers agreed to provide a banner embroidered with the crest of the company, a refectory table and a set of 12 chairs, all of Warwickshire oak. The master's chair, 11 other chairs and a table were designed by Spence at an estimated cost of £364.17s.9d. There would also be a replacement for the 1914-18 war memorial. A replacement for the banner embroidered by the Royal School of Needlework was rejected on the grounds of excessive cost (£1500-£2000) and instead Spence suggested tapestry by an Edinburgh company at £360.

When Spence's design was shown in 1957, 'some doubt was at first expressed about the brightness of the red background, the rather ornate design of the red mantling, the flesh colour of the hand and arm, and the drama of the helmet'. Fortunately, these objections were withdrawn, and in December 1957 the Bishop of Coventry came at the invitation of the gild to dedicate their new Cappers' Room. This continues to be used for meetings on a regular basis.

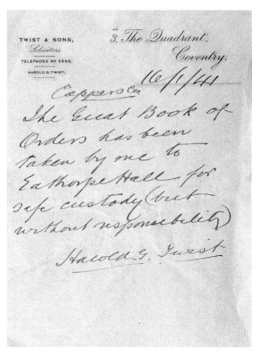

One of the great thinkers of the post-war age, born in Coventry, was Frank Whittle, who at the age of nine moved to Leamington, where he became a scholarship boy at Leamington College. Whittle developed the jet engine; this can with justice be said to have changed the direction of the twentieth century. He was not, however, the first

A relic of the Cappers' archive, 'the Great Book of Orders', was saved from the bombing by Harold Twist in 1941.

Coventry product to have selected aviation for study. As early as 1907-8 Frederick Lanchester had published important theoretical studies on aerial flight, though these were not taken up by the aeronautical establishment. Even earlier, in 1890, in the factory of a hollow-fork manufacturer (Richardson describes it as in 'one of those streets with a mixture of small houses and factories which have played such an important part in the city's industrial development') an attempt was made to build an ornithopter with two enormous oscillating wings powered by electricity and designed by a Major R.F. Moore. Another pioneer, W.A. Weaver, also constructed an ornithopter said to have risen to a height of 50ft over Hampton-in-Arden golf course in 1906. Weaver was a friend of John Siddeley, later Lord Kenilworth, another Coventry magnate who became involved in aviation. Siddeley, who seems to have had all the qualifications, was never a Capper.

Aviation did not establish any permanent home in Coventry – the industry lost over 11,000 jobs in the city in the five years up to 1967, while in the same period the increase in employment in the car industry ensured greater dependency on road vehicle and accessory manufacture. Five Lord Mayor's conferences were held in 1968 to discuss with political leaders and representatives of industry 'from both sides' (as it was put in those days) the problems which would face the city if it did not attract a wider range of industries to revive its ageing factory plant and buildings. There was also the difficulty that the city offered very little employment to office workers in the service industries.

These mayoral conferences, though they perhaps did not result in measurable change in the city, illustrate that the mayor's office was not a sinecure. Indeed it was often held by men who, as suggested

earlier, had a deeply felt charitable instinct. One of them was a notable Capper, Sir William Wyley (1852-1940). His family, which in the 18th century

Thanks to the efforts of Percy Martin, the aero-engine industry (featuring plant like this Bentley rotary) was established in Coventry for the duration of World War I.

had established a chemist's business, had become so prosperous that he was not only sent to Rugby school, but later to Paris to study business methods so that he could return to Coventry to apply these at the family firm, of which he eventually became managing director. He built for himself a fine mansion out of the ruins of the former Carthusian monastery guesthouse along the London Road.

Richardson cites Wyley's various public duties and charitable works. He joined the Volunteers and the Territorials and in 1938 was knighted for his work for the city's churches and on the city council. When he first joined the latter in 1876, Richardson says 'he was one of the rising young men deeply influenced by the contemporary interest in public health questions.... He advocated purchase of

A group photograph features some of the women 'aero-engine strippers' who worked at the Siddeley-Darley plant until the end of World War I.

the gasworks, secured the appointment of a Public Analyst... and the extension of the Isolation Hospital... before he retired in 1888, his connection with the council had almost been forgotten 'when, in 1911, he was invited to accept the Mayoralty'. He helped create a museum, gave Cook Street Gate to the city in 1913, and, on his death, left the city his house and lands at Charterhouse. Wyley had been master of the Cappers in 1914, and again in 1931-2.

The Wyley family were manufacturing chemists by profession and shortly before the 1939 war William Wyley was knighted for his services to Coventry. Also knighted for services to the city was Charles Barratt, a lawyer who was coaxed to Coventry in 1941 as deputy town clerk, and although not a capper himself was much concerned with the creation of the University of Warwick through the 1950s and '60s.

Education was, of course, a pre-occupation of many a Victorian philanthropist. In 1803 John and Alexander Rotherham, both

Cappers, joined with a number of other employers to start a movement which was to lead to the creation of the Coventry Technical Institute. This opened its doors in 1887, though it had yet to recruit any full-time staff. Its object was to provide a continuing training for the working-class student who had left full-time education too soon. A more recent example of a Capper's interest in education was the appointment of Sir William Wyley to chairman of the governors of King Henry VIII grammar school. A distinguished Capper who attended this school was R.S. Rudland, later appointed Hon. Physician to the Queen, and a trustee of various charities.

Culture is a rather broader concept than education, and the former was the pre-occupation of the son and successor of Samuel Theo, Samuel H. Newsome. He believed that he had a responsibility for the cultural life of the city. But this was, he thought, in a straightjacket because of the considerable size of the Coventry Theatre, which had to be filled with a popular audience if it were to pay its way. To meet the post-war demand for music and ballet, he introduced there the Covent Garden touring opera and similar companies.

More recently, Cappers and their families have contributed to the cultural life of the city in various ways. The son of Percy Martin, for example, made a notable contribution to that major development, Warwick University, which has acheived worldwide recognition for artistic as well as academic excellence, progressing in drama, art, music, opera, film and other media. The heritage of the mystery plays has not, after all, faded away.

For a city to flourish culturally it needs the support of business, and Coventry has attracted major administrative or headquarter complexes from such large instituitions as Barclays Bank, Marconi, PowerGen and National Grid.

This meal at the annual Capper
Bean Feast emphasise the simple fare
which in former times made up the
main diet of their less fortunate
brethren in the city. This would
inspire them, from the 19th century,
to concentrate gild activity more
and more on charitable works.

This book was written in the year 2000. Its beginnings deal with the early days of hat manufacture in the years around 1400. A halfway point between the years when the Cappers were active, and the present day, would therefore be about 1700. This was the period when Daniel Defoe wrote his *Tour through the Whole Island of Great Britain* In it he describes how this city was notorious for producing riots at election times, when the inhabitants fought pitched battles in the streets, conducted not only by the 'scum and rabble' but also by the ordinary citizens. From time-to-time complaints of loutish behaviour are repeated today.

Defoe also described it as 'a large and populous city [which] drives a very great trade; the manufacture of tammies is their chief employ.... The buildings are very old, and in some places much decayed'. Present day Coventry can still be described as 'large and populous', though in fact its numbers are in moderate decline. Defoe's strictures on the state of the 18th-century buildings would not bear repetition, as the city fathers and their friends have been assiduous in the rebuilding and restoring of many fine old buildings. In particular many individual Cappers have supported a major fund-raising project to raise endowments to maintain the Cathedral's fabric through the Development Fund. The latter, too, regulary uses the Cappers' Room for fund-raising events of one kind and another.

As they contemplate these messages of the Millennium, the Cappers of the year 2000 have some tangible evidence to assist them in forming judgements about the changes which their ancient company has undergone over the past 600 years; they can take satisfaction, too, from the knowledge that they have retained their identity when so many others have lost theirs.

EPILOGUE

'A VERY SPECIAL BEAN FEAST'

The Master of the Cappers in 1998, the present Lord Iliffe, wanted to mark the passing of the years since his grandfather, the 1st Baron Iliffe and likewise Master of the Cappers, had held a Bean Feast at his home, Yattendon, and simultaneously to make preparations for marking the Millennium which would follow two years later.

He therefore requested a Bean Feast to be held at Yattendon on 4th July 1998, 65 years to the month after that called on 27th July 1933 by his grandfather, which had been attended by an illustrious group of 11 members, namely 'Esquires Kevitt Rotherham, Percy Martin, Charles Browett, Hugh Rotherham, Harold Twist, Crosbie Dawson, Maurice Lorrimer, Ewan Rotherham, William Wyley, Walter Browett, Nelson Smith'. A group of similar distinction attended in 1998.

At an appropriate moment during the feast, the Master presented to the Fellowship 12 hats made by Miss Nicola de Selincourt, Hatter and Milliner. These hats represented hat design and fashion over the last 500 years, and Lord Iliffe expressed the hope that they would be displayed at the Company's headquarters, known as the Cappers' Room and situated within the walls of the ruins of Coventry Cathedral, in order to mark the Millennium. Subsequently the hats were photographed by Florence Kipling daughter of the then Master and are reproduced here for the first time.

1450 – 1500
Brown felt.

1500 – 1550
Feather and brooch trim, on felt
or velvet.

1550 – 1600
Hunting hat of beaver and
peacock feathers.

1600 – 1650
Beaver hat with jewelled band and
ostrich feathers.

1650 – 1700
Wide-brimmed hat trimmed
with feathers.

1700 – 1750
Up-turned brim with leather sides
(brown).

1750 – 1800
Tall-crowned navy felt with narrow
turned-up brim.

1800 – 1850
Black top hat.

1850 – 1900
Bowler.

1900 – 1950
Felt trilby with feather trim.

1950 – 2000
A man's 'pork-pie' with the
inevitable feather

2000
Futuristic hat.

Appendix I

The felt-hatting industry, c. 1500-1850

(WITH PARTICULAR REFERENCE
TO LANCASHIRE AND CHESHIRE)

BY MISS P.M. GILES M.A.

In the Middle Ages caps of knitted wool were a common form of headgear. The earliest reference so far traced to their manufacture is a set of ordinances dated 1258, belonging to the craft of Cappers in the City of London. These include the regulation that no-one should 'make a cap except of good white or grey wool or black... Also that no-one shall cause an old cap to be dyed black for selling again, because when exposed 'to the rain it falls to pieces'. Some seventy years later, in 1328, among those elected in 'divers misteries of London' were numbered the 'Haberdassheres', not craftsmen, but merchants either of small wares or of all manner of headgear. Thirdly, in 1347 the Hatters' Company of London was incorporated. It is not yet known, however, whether the hatters of 1347 worked in felt. It is probably correct to say that felt hats were not extensively manufactured in England for general use before the sixteenth century. As a luxury article these had been imported from Bruges, France, and Milan (hence the term 'millinery'). Early in the reign of Henry VIII immigrants from the first two countries caused an expansion of the industry, and by 1576 there were about 400 native-born feltmakers in and about London.

The new type of hat, both foreign and English made, proved a serious rival to the old-established capping industry. In 1565 the

Cappers were complaining of an 'excessive use of hats and felts, causing the impoverishment and decay of great multitudes making woollen caps, ... bringing good cities and towns to desolation'. In fact no fewer than five statutes were passed between 1511 and 1570 to protect the Cappers. In the latter year Parliament ruled that every male person, not possessed of a rental of 20 marks a year, should wear on the Sunday or holyday a cap of wool wrought in England, under penalty of a fine of 3s.4d. But such legislation failed to check the well-to-do, who indulged more and more, as the puritanical Philip Stubbes complained in 1583, in hats of velvet, taffeta, sarsenet, or 'of a certain kinde of fine hair. These thei call Bever hattes of xx, xxx or xl shillings price, fetched from beyond the seas'. Chaucer's Prologue has a much earlier reference to a 'Flaundrish bever hat'. The Elizabethan beavers, however, may well have been imported not only from Flanders but also direct from Spain, where there was a flourishing hatting industry in the sixteenth century. Later, the famous trip of Prince Charles and the Duke of Buckingham to Spain to woo the Spanish Infanta doubtless increased the popularity of the beaver hat and its manufacture in England, until its wear became universal among the upper classes.

During the Stuart period, it was decided by whom the new industry should be controlled in the capital. At first the London haberdashers seemed clearly marked out for leadership. In 1502 these had succeeded in absorbing both the Cappers' and Hatters' Companies. In later Tudor and early Stuart times, the haberdashers formed one of the wealthier London companies, occupying 'large, fayre and beautiful buildings' on London Bridge and the 'south side of the Poultrie'. But they were unpopular: denounced as 'rich men' bent on the 'destruction of pore people'. Their attempt to control the supply of raw materials for felt-hatting as well as the distribution of the finished product, brought them into conflict with the increasing body of artisan feltmakers. These latter were at a disadvantage, denied effectual representation in the haberdashers, yet having, as they said, 'no government of themselves as other companies have'. Nevertheless, the future lay with the feltmakers, partly because the haberdashers were considered merely traders, whereas 'the feltmakers we must cherish well', since they alone 'by their misteries and faculties doe bring in anie treasour'. Thus, when the latter made application to the crown for a charter conferring on them the sole right to regulate their craft, it was granted by James I in 1604. The struggle was not finally ended for another half century. During this period the haberdashers were strong enough to prevent the feltmakers from obtaining recognition as one of the Livery Companies, which alone could confer the freedom of the City. By 1667, however, with the confirmation of their charter by Charles II, the control of the trade had passed into the hands of the feltmakers, and the haberdashers practically disappeared from the scene.

Meanwhile, in provincial centres of hatting such as Bristol, Exeter, Kendal and Ripon, the haberdashers and feltmakers were associated on a more equal and friendlier footing, which doubtless proved an advantage over the London situation in the development of the industry. Friendliness, however, was not the keynote of their relations at Chester. Here the feltmakers had joined the skinners, and the amalgamated company kept a watchful eye on all haberdashers' activities, insisting that the latter should confine their sales to straw hats. The development of felt-hatting in provincial centres, though widespread, was confined during the seventeenth and early eighteenth centuries to the coarser felts of wool and coney then worn both by men and 'women of inferior quality'. The expensive beaver hats, requiring greater skill and good taste in production, were still made only in London. Clearly some provincial centres had arisen near local supplies of wool, as at Bristol and Kendal. The earliest reference to feltmakers at Chester is 1629, at Coventry, 1636. Newcastle-under-Lyme was an important centre during the seventeenth century, where there were stated to be 'great numbers of master-hatters employing 9 to 10 journeymen each'. In Lancashire, Warrington was of some importance, and Manchester was making coarse felt hats in the latter part of the century. At Oldham a master-hatter is named in 1654, though the development of hatting as the staple industry of the town dates only from the eighteenth century, associated with the firm of Clegg. At Preston there were hatters in the late seventeenth century, as we know from William Stout. Here a hatter named John Powell, 'a litigious man, of the Presbyterian religion, very much envied the drapers for their selling hats, as not belonging to their trade; and they so much envying him for meddling with them in such an impertinence, and partly for his pretended sanctity in religion'. Powell was, in fact, the leader of the common freemen who sympathised with the cause of the Duke of Monmouth, against the drapers and the governing party supporting James II. Trade, religion and politics, both local and national, were here closely intermingled.

In the corporate boroughs, as in London, the hatting industry was controlled by craft gilds whose jurisdiction extended from three to four miles beyond the borough boundary. Within this area none but a freeman could work, though interlopers, 'foreigners', were constantly trying to do so. In Chester, for example, the skinners and feltmakers conducted a lengthy lawsuit, from 1731 to 1740, against Zachariah Smith, who, not being a freeman, set up as a master hatter in the city. The company finally triumphed, and was permitted to pull down and carry off the tools of the interloper's trade. The London company was scarcely well established when the City was overtaken by the twin disasters of plague and fire. Though numerous, the feltmakers were stated to be 'not of so great ability as most of the other companies in London... when the great sickness raged, and count not retire into the country as the more wealthy sort of people did'. Such numbers were therefore 'swept off' that the remnant was obliged to admit a host of foreigners. The normal procedure of the London company was, however, as that at Chester, strengthened in 1757 by an Act of the Common Council, permitting appeal to the Lord Mayor's Court to enforce their ordinance.

The numerous foreign master hatters, in the suburbs, in country districts, and in growing industrial centres such as Manchester and Birmingham – mere manorial boroughs – had, it is true, lower standard of workmanship, but they could also pay their foreign journeymen considerably lower wages. By one of their ordinances, the City masters were forbidden to employ these foreign journeymen: an ordinance it was clearly in the interests of the London journeymen to maintain. In 1678, for example, six journeymen attended the Feltmakers' Court to charge a hatter with employing foreigners and refusing work to freemen. Their privileged status would be endangered if the large reservoir of country labour could be freely drawn upon. It included women, children not regularly apprenticed and many of both sexes – 100,000 according to one exaggerated report – become dependent on charity at the close of the seventeenth century on account of the declining use of coarse felts. In the next fifty years, however, it became clear that the old system, relating to the journeymen at least, was doomed. By 1750 it was calculated that the London feltmakers employed more foreigners than freemen. The clerk of the company himself admitted in 1752 to employing foreigners to freemen in the proportion of six to one. In 1755 the company legalised its position by repealing the restrictive ordinance forbidding the employment of foreigners, an important action marking the general decline of the gild system in the capital. Within the next decade many feltmakers of London used their legal freedom to expand by establishing factories in the north of England, where, as they explained, wages were so much lower.

This eighteenth-century expansion would not have been possible without a series of vitally important steps by which the industry ensured its supplies of raw material for home and abroad, and secured itself against overseas competition, to attain finally a position of virtual monopoly. Here again, the London Feltmakers' Company invariably played the leading rôle.

During the seventeenth century the home market expanded with the aid of a heavy tariff against imported hats. By the early eighteenth century a large export trade had also developed to Spain, Portugal, Italy, Germany, and in fact most European countries. The greatest part of the beaver was obtained from the territory of the Hudson's Bay Company, but there was also an import from most of the colonies on the Atlantic seaboard, to which in return we exported the beaver hats. The colonists, however, especially in New England and New York, now began 'notwithstanding any law to the contrary' to manufacture their own hats, cheaper since escaping the 6d. duty on skins imported to England. They also took advantage of short apprenticeships, and employed negro labour. As a result the English found they were being undersold by as much as 5s. a hat in the colonies. Worse still, colonial hats were being exported to the Spanish and West Indies, to Ireland and even to the mother country itself.

Early in 1732, the Feltmakers' Company decided to take action, and in the same year obtained, at their own expense, an act forbidding these irregularities. This laid down that the colonists must observe the seven year apprenticeship regulation, while it prohibited the use of negro labour and forbade entirely the export of their hats. The act, however, was not altogether successful. It did restrict manufacture to some extent in New York, but elsewhere, especially in New England, its provisions were large evaded. The colonists, however, continued to import from England their superior quality hats for town wear, and their value as customers did not seriously decline until the early nineteenth century and their successful introduction of machinery in the eighteen forties.

Undoubtedly the far more serious eighteenth century rival was

France, the only other possessor of the North American beaver lands. Earlier French competition had appeared to receive a mortal blow with the Revocation of the Edict of Nantes in 1685. Despite serious alarm caused to the Feltmakers' Company, the English hatting industry had benefited more than any other by the influx of industrious Huguenots. They settled, outside the company's jurisdiction, at Wandsworth, Battersea, and Lambeth, where they set up large factories to make the best quality beaver hats. Not only their skill was lost to France, but also a secret recipe for the liquid used in preparing skins. It seems rather singular that five years after this self-inflicted blow the French government should have imposed a crippling tax on their own hats. This alone, according to Stephen Dowell, caused the final complete collapse of French competition. But his assertion is far from correct, since during the succeeding half-century the French managed to regain much of their former reputation for hatting. After forty years a Frenchman named Mathiez is said to have stolen from London and thus restored to his country the lost secret of the trade. Foreign labour was cheaper than English, and by 1750 the French Canada Company was reputed to be importing far more beaver than Great Britain. Moreover, British fur-dealers were encouraged by a drawback on the 6d. duty to re-export skins, especially to Holland and Flanders. The skins were considered superior to those of the French Canada Company; and in any case the French dealers were forbidden to re-export. Thus by 1750 the English hatters were complaining of a shortage of raw materials and inability to employ their journeymen, while the French had become 'our greatest and most dangerous rivals', their hats now 'held in higher reputation than English'.

Again the London Feltmakers' Company took the initiative. On 7 January 1751 the members decided to apply to Parliament for an act to prohibit the re-export of beaver, over £400 being subscribed for this purpose. But a deputation waiting upon Lord Pelham was obliged to confess two months later that it had received no great encouragement.

Seeking public support, both the feltmakers and the Hudson's Bay Company resorted to pamphleteering. While the latter feared a restriction of trade if the English hatters could not absorb the entire cargo of fur, the hatters pleaded that their case was as strong as that of the woollen manufacturers in whose interests the export of wool was prohibited. For the time being, however, they were defeated, nor did a second committee formed in the December of the same year meet with any better success.

Within the next decade, if the feltmakers' evidence is to be believed, English exports declined still further with the total loss of the Spanish and Portuguese markets. While the value of all exports of beaver hats decreased to less than half, in some years the re-export of beaver-skins exceeded the import. The feltmakers, though not relaxing their representations to the government, were unsuccessful once again in 1759. But by 1763 the situation had been completely transformed by the fortunes of war. By the transfer of Canada to English hands, this country now possessed all the North American beaver lands.

In January 1763 the Government informed the feltmakers that it wished 'to render the conquest of Canada more important and useful to this kingdom by taking off the drawback on Beaver and giving all reasonable encouragement to the Beaver Hat manufacture'. The Feltmakers needed no second hint, and a committee immediately waited upon Lord Bute with a memorial. Even so, Bute dared not precipitate matters without, as he said, first consulting the Hudson's Bay Company. Another twelve month passed, after which the Committee was able to demonstrate, at a conference with the Treasury Board, that beaver was being purchased by France; whereupon the Board recommended a petition to Parliament. It was thus with government approval that the Feltmakers once again took steps to obtain the desired act. This time they also sought and gained the close co-operation not only of their own journeymen, but also of hatters in Manchester and district, Chester, Liverpool, Newcastle-under-Lyme and Bristol, whence petitions modelled on their own were sent to the House of Commons. Prominent master hatters laid their evidence before a Parliamentary Committee, and despite 'great opposition', the bill became law on 5 April 1764. With the substitution of a duty for the drawback on re-export of beaver, English hatters had now ensured, as they thought, a lastingly adequate supply of the best quality skins. No sooner, however, had the Feltmakers' Committee safely shepherded this project through Parliament, than serious alarm was taken in the following year at the passage of an apparently favourable bill to prevent poaching in fishponds and rabbit warrens. Beaver was too expensive for many hats to be made of it entirely, at least by mid-eighteenth century. Instead, the body was made of a varying mixture of wool and rabbits' or hares' fur, to which a beaver nap was applied.

Thus, to the hatting industry, English rabbit-warrens provided an indispensable source of raw material, superior to any imported, for best 'bodies' and 'the castor, or middling sort of hat'. The protection this bill intended to afford was, however, rendered uncertain by exempting from its provisions sea banks and walls of tidal estuaries. Such general exemption, the Feltmakers considered, would lead to 'the demolition of all rabbits'. Hastily the Committee despatched a petition, seconded by one from Manchester hatters, against the bill as it stood, lobbied M.P.s on the subject, and submitted to the Treasury Lords a revised clause exempting only the coastal defence of Lincolnshire, which they admitted to have been seriously weakened by rabbits' excavations. The Committee, finally had the satisfaction of reporting that the modified act 'favoured the culture of rabbits in every possible way'.

A few finishing touches rendered the position completely secure. Two or three years later, the Feltmakers obtained a heavy duty, imposed by Charles Townshend, of 6s. a dozen on French straw hats, and 6s. a pound on straw plaiting for their manufacture in England.

Some years later, the supply of English rabbits' and hares' fur was again threatened, this time by export to our potential rivals, France, Flanders and America. The action of the trade was again successful, and an act secured in July 1784, forbidding the export of these commodities, while at the same time the import of goats' wool from the Levant was freed from duty.

This action is important, incidentally, as indicating that the leadership of the industry was passing into other hands. It was the hatters of London, Westminster and Southwark who formed an association distinct from the Feltmakers' Company to approach the House of Commons. To this move the Skinners' and Feltmakers' Company of Chester lent their aid, financial and otherwise. But the London Feltmakers, when invited, declined to give their support in any way, since, they said, they had not been consulted. The preceding year they had been moved to deplore the neglect and impoverishment of their company's interests, 'impaired, declined, and fallen to decay', its byelaws 'likely to come into contempt'. By 1800, despite efforts to revive their authority, the Feltmakers had little left to consider save the administration of their charities and their annual dinner.

An industry now so protected and flourishing appeared to the Younger Pitt a suitable object for taxation. In his 1784 budget Pitt added hats to a long list of new taxes. The hat tax rose from 3d. on a hat 4s. in value, to 2s. on a hat costing above 12s.; it was imposed by means of a stamp on the lining, and paid by the customer as a separate item on the bill. In its first year, the tax yielded £60,000. But by 1811, Spencer Perceval, in his budget speech, said he had found 'the tax... to be the uniform subject of complaint', since the evasion was connived at by dealers and purchasers alike. By this time the tax yielded less than half of £60,000, and, being both unprofitable and impractical, was repealed.

Appendix II

THE CAPPERS COMPANY: MASTERS AND MEMBERS 1900-2000

Year of Office	Master	Members
1900/1901	George Francis Twist	John Gulson, John Rotherham, Francis William Franklin, Montague S. Wilks, Arthur Seymour, Fred Twist, James Marriott, Arthur E. Jagger, William Hillman, J. G. C. Graham, Harold Smith, George Singer, Denis McVeagh, Alex Rotherham, John Powers
1901/1902	William Hillman	No change
1902/1903	James George Collins	John Gulson, John Rotherham, Francis William Franklin, Denis McVeagh, Fred Twist, James Marriott, George F. Twist, Montague S. Wilks, Arthur Seymour, John Powers, Harold Smith, George Singer, Arthur E. Jagger, William Hillman, J. G. C. Graham
1903/1904	John Gulson	No change
1904/1905	Arthur Seymour	John Rotherham, Francis William Franklin, Denis McVeagh, Fred Twist, James Marriott, George F. Twist, Montague S. Wilks, Arthur Seymour, John Powers, Harold Smith, George Singer, Arthur E. Jagger, William Hillman, J. G. C. Graham, Kevitt Rotherham
1905/1906	Kevitt Rotherham	Francis William Franklin, Denis McVeagh, Fred Twist, James Marriott, George Singer, Montague S. Wilks, Arthur Seymour, John Powers, Harold Smith, Arthur E. Jagger, William Hillman, J. G. C. Graham, George F. Twist
1906/1907	John Powers	Francis William Franklin, Denis McVeagh, Fred Twist, Harold Smith, George Singer, Montague S. Wilks, Arthur Seymour, J. G. C. Graham, Kevitt Rotherham, Walter Browett, Arthur E. Jagger, William Hillman, James Marriott, George F. Twist
1907/1908	Harold Smith	Francis William Franklin, Walter Browett, Arthur E. Jagger, George F. Twist, Kevitt Rotherham, Denis McVeagh, Fred Twist, James Marriott, George Singer, Arthur Seymour, John Powers, William Hillman, J. G. C. Graham

Year				
1908/1909	Walter Browett	Francis William Franklin Denis McVeagh Fred Twist George F. Twist	Arthur Seymour John Powers Harold Smith Arthur E. Jagger	William Hillman J. G. C. Graham Kevitt Rotherham
1909/1910	Arthur Edward Jagger		No change	
1910/1911	William Hillman		No change	
1911/1912	J. G. C. Graham	Francis William Franklin Denis McVeagh Fred Twist George F Twist Arthur Seymour	John Powers Harold Smith Arthur E. Jagger William Hillman William F. Wyley	Walter Browett Alan Rotherham William Thackhall Browett Hugh Rotherham Kevitt Rotherham
1912/1913	Alexander Rotherham	Francis William Franklin William Hillman J. G. C. Graham Kevitt Rotherham Walter Browett	Arthur E. Jagger William Thackhall Browett Hugh Rotherham William F. Wyley	Denis McVeagh Fred Twist John Powers Harold Smith
1913/1914	Hugh Rotherham	Fred Twist John Powers Harold Smith Arthur E. Jagger	William Hillman J. G. C. Graham Kevitt Rotherham Walter Browett	Alex Rotherham William Thackhall Browett Hugh Rotherham William F. Wyley
1914/1915	William Fitzthomas Wyley	Fred Twist Walter Browett Alex Rotherham William Thackhall Browett Hugh Rotherham	Kevitt Rotherham Edward Mauger Iliffe Maurice Lorrimer Ewan Rotherham Harold Godfrey Twist	John Powers Arthur E. Jagger William Hillman J. G. C. Graham
1915/1916	William Thackhall Browett		No change	
1916/1917	Edward Mauger Iliffe		No change	
1917/1918	Edward Mauger Iliffe		No change	
1918/1919	Edward Mauger Iliffe		No change	
1919/1920	Maurice Lorrimer	Fred Twist William Hillman William Thackhall Browett Hugh Rotherham	Walter Browett Alex Rotherham Ewan Rotherham Harold Godfrey Twist	Edward Mauger Iliffe J. G. C. Graham Kevitt Rotherham William F. Wyley

Year of Office	Master	Members		
1920/1921	Ewan Rotherham	J. G. C. Graham Kevitt Rotherham Walter Browett Alex Rotherham Harold Godfrey Twist	Hugh Rotherham William F. Wyley Edward Mauger Iliffe Maurice Lorrimer Percy Martin	Harold Nelson Smith G. Crosbie Dawson R. A. Rotherham A. P. Pridmore William Thackhall Browett
1921/1922	Harold Godfrey Twist		No change	
1922/1923	Harold Nelson Smith	J. G. C. Graham Sir Edward Iliffe Maurice Lorrimer William Thackhall Browett Hugh Rotherham	William F. Wyley G. Crosbie Dawson R. A. Rotherham Ewan Rotherham Harold Godfrey Twist	Kevitt Rotherham Walter Browett A. P. Pridmore Percy Martin
1923/1924	George Crosbie Dawson	Kevitt Rotherham Maurice Lorrimer Ewan Rotherham Harold Godfrey Twist H. Nelson Smith	Sir Edward Iliffe R. A. Rotherham A. P. Pridmore Percy Martin	Walter Browett William Thackhall Browett Hugh Rotherham William F. Wyley
1924/1925	R. Alexander Rotherham	Keith Rotherham Walter Browett Ewan Rotherham Harold G. Twist	Sir Edward Iliffe Maurice Lorrimer A. P. Pridmore Percy Martin	G. Crosbie Dawson Hugh Rotherham William F. Wyley H. Nelson Smith
1925/1926	Alexander Percy Pridmore	Kevitt Rotherham Walter Browett Hugh Rotherham William F. Wyley	Sir Edward Iliffe Maurice Lorrimer Ewan Rotherham Harold G. Twist H. Nelson Smith	G. Crosbie Dawson R. A. Rotherham A. P. Pridmore Percy Martin
1926/1927	Percy Martin		No change	
1927/1928	Kevitt Rotherham		No change	
1928/1929	Walter Browett	Kevitt Rotherham Walter Browett Hugh Rotherham William F. Wyley	Sir Edward Iliffe Maurice Lorrimer Ewan Rotherham Harold G. Twist H. Nelson Smith	G. Crosbie Dawson A. P. Pridmore Percy Martin Charles Browett

Year				
1929/1930	Hugh Rotherham		No change	
1930/1931	Charles Browett		No change	
1931/1932	William Fitzthomas Wyley		No change	
1932/1933	The Lord Iliffe) (1st Baron Iliffe)	Kevitt Rotherham Walter Browett Hugh Rotherham William F. Wyley	The Lord Iliffe Maurice Lorrimer Ewan Rotherham Harold G. Twist H. Nelson Smith	G. Crosbie Dawson A. P. Pridmore Percy Martin Charles Browett
1933/1934	Maurice Lorrimer		No change	
1934/1935	Ewan Rotherham		No change	
1935/1936	Harold G. Twist	Kevitt Rotherham Hugh Rotherham William F. Wyley The Lord Iliffe	Maurice Lorrimer Ewan Rotherham Harold G. Twist H. Nelson Smith	G. Crosbie Dawson A. P. Pridmore Percy Martin Charles Browett
1936/1937	Harold Nelson Smith		No change	
1937/1938	George Crosbie Dawson		No change	
1938/1939	Alexander Percy Pridmore	Kevitt Rotherham Sir William F. Wyley The Lord Iliffe Maurice Lorrimer	Ewan Rotherham Harold G. Twist H. Nelson Smith	G. Crosbie Dawson A. P. Pridmore Percy Martin Charles Browett
1939/1940	Percy Martin	Kevitt Rotherham Sir William F. Wyley The Lord Iliffe Maurice Lorrimer	Ewan Rotherham Harold G. Twist H. Nelson Smith A. P. Pridmore	Percy Martin Charles Browett The Hon. Langton Iliffe Col. R. J. Cash MC
1940/1941	Charles Browett		No change	
1941/1942	F/Lt The Hon. Langton Iliffe	Kevitt Rotherham The Lord Iliffe Maurice Lorrimer Ewan Rotherham	Harold G. Twist H. Nelson Smith A. P. Pridmore Percy Martin	Charles Browett F/Lt The Hon. Langton Iliffe Col. R. J. Cash CBE MC A. H. Jagger Major The Lord Leigh
1942/1943	F/Lt The Hon. Langton Iliffe	Kevitt Rotherham The Lord Iliffe Maurice Lorrimer	A. P. Pridmore Percy Martin Charles Browett	F/Lt The Hon. Langton Iliffe Col. R. J. Cash CBE MC A. H. Jagger Major The Lord Leigh

Year of Office	Master	Members		
1943/1944	F/Lt The Hon. Langton Iliffe	No change		
1944/1945	Col. Reginald John Cash CBE MC	Kevitt Rotherham The Lord Iliffe Maurice Lorrimer	A. P. Pridmore Percy Martin The Hon. Langton Iliffe P. H. V. Twist	Col. R. J. Cash CBE MC A. H. Jagger The Lord Leigh
1945/1946	The Hon. Langton Iliffe	No change		
1946/1947	Arthur Humphrey Jagger	Kevitt Rotherham The Lord Iliffe Maurice Lorrimer S. H. Newsome	Percy Martin The Hon. Langton Iliffe Col. R. J. Cash CBE MC	A. H. Jagger The Lord Leigh P. H. V. Twist The Lord Norton
1947/1948	Major The Lord Leigh	No change		
1948/1949	Samuel H. Newsome	No change		
1949/1950	The Lord Iliffe (2nd Baron Iliffe)	The Lord Iliffe Maurice Lorrimer Percy Martin The Lord Norton	The Hon. Langton Iliffe Col. R. J. Cash CBE MC A. H. Jagger	The Lord Leigh P. H. V. Twist S. H. Newsome Julian Hoare
1950/1951	Percy Martin	The Lord Iliffe Maurice Lorrimer Percy Martin The Hon. Langton Iliffe	Col. R. J. Cash CBE MC A. H. Jagger The Lord Leigh P.H.V. Twist P. S. Rendall	S. H. Newsome Julian Hoare W. Lyons A. J. Newsome
1951/1952	Percy Martin	No change		
1952/1953	Patrick Hare Vivian Twist	No change		
1953/1954	Julian Hoare	The Lord Iliffe A. H. Jagger The Lord Leigh P. H. V. Twist	Col. R. J. Cash CB CBE MC Julian Hoare W. Lyons A. J. Newsome	S. H. Newsome Percy Martin The Hon. Langton Iliffe P. S. Rendall

Year				
1954/1955	Alan Newsome	The Lord Iliffe Percy Martin The Hon. Langton Iliffe Col. R. J. Cash CB CBE MC	The Lord Leigh A. H. Jagger P. H. V. Twist P. S. Rendall	S. H. Newsome Julian Hoare Sir William Lyons A. J. Newsome
1955/1956	Sir William Lyons		No change	
1956/1957	Philip Stanley Rendall		No change	
1957/1958	Col. Sir Reginald John Cash KBE, CB, MC	The Lord Iliffe Percy Martin The Hon. Langton Iliffe Col. Sir Reginald Cash KBE CB MC	The Lord Leigh A. H. Jagger P. H. V. Twist P. S. Rendall	S. H. Newsome Julian Hoare Sir William Lyons A. J. Newsome
1958/1959	The Hon. Langton Iliffe	The Lord Iliffe S. H. Newsome A. H. Jagger	S. Rendall The Lord Leigh Sir William Lyons A. J. Newsome	The Hon. Langton Iliffe Julian Hoare P. H. V. Twist
1959/1960	Arthur Humphrey Jagger	The Lord Iliffe (2nd Baron Iliffe) Sir William Lyons P. S. Rendall	Sir Stanley Harley Julian Hoare A. H. Jagger Dr J. Vaughan Bradley MBE	The Lord Leigh A. J. Newsome S. H. Newsome P. H. V. Twist
1960/1961	Major The Lord Leigh		No change	
1961/1962	Dr. John Vaughan Bradley	The Lord Iliffe S. H. Newsome Sir Stanley Harley	Sir William Lyons Dr. J. Vaughan Bradley MBE Julian Hoare P. S. Rendall	The Lord Leigh P. H. V. Twist The Earl of Aylesford
1962/1963	Sir Stanley Harley	The Lord Iliffe Dr. J. Vaughan Bradley MBE	Sir William Lyons Julian Hoare	P. H. V. Twist The Earl of Aylesford
1963/1964	The 11th Earl of Aylesford	The Lord Iliffe A. J. Newsome S. H. Newsome P. S. Rendall	Sir William Lyons P. H. V. Twist Sir Stanley Harley Dr. R. S. Rudland	The Lord Leigh Dr. J. Vaughan Bradley MBE Julian Hoare The Earl of Aylesford
1964/1965	Surgeon Captain Robert Spencer Rudland VRD, RNR		No change	

Year of Office	Master	Members		
1965/1966	Samuel H. Newsome	No change		
1966/1967	Patrick Hare Vivian Twist	The Lord Iliffe S. H. Newsome Dr. J. Vaughan Bradley MBE	Sir William Lyons Sir Stanley Harley Dr. R. S. Rudland MBE	P. H. V. Twist P. S. Rendall MBE
1967/1968	Julian Hoare	The Lord Iliffe A. J. Newsome S. H. Newsome P. S. Rendall MBE	Sir William Lyons P. H. V. Twist Sir Stanley Harley Dr. R. S. Rudland MBE	The Lord Leigh Dr. J. Vaughan Bradley MBE Julian Hoare The Earl of Aylesford
1968/1969	Alan J. Newsome	No change		
1969/1970	Sir William Lyons	The Lord Iliffe A. J. Newsome Julian Hoare Dr. R. S. Rudland MBE	Sir William Lyons P. H. V. Twist Sir Stanley Harley	The Lord Leigh Dr. J. Vaughan Bradley MBE P. S. Rendall MBE The Earl of Aylesford
1970/1971	Philip Stanley Rendall	No change		
1971/1972	The Lord Iliffe	The Lord Iliffe Dr. R. S. Rudland MBE Sir Stanley Harley A. J. Newsome	Julian Hoare The Lord Leigh R. P. R. Iliffe	Dr. J. Vaughan Bradley MBE Sir William Lyons P. H. V. Twist The Earl of Aylesford
1972/1973	The Lord Leigh	The Lord Iliffe The Lord Leigh A. J. Newsome Sir Stanley Harley	P. S. Rendall MBE Sir William Lyons Dr. R. S. Rudland MBE	The Earl of Aylesford P. H. V. Twist Julian Hoare R. P. R. Iliffe
1973/1974	Sir Stanley Harley	The Lord Iliffe The Lord Leigh P. H. V. Twist Julian Hoare	P. S. Rendall MBE Sir William Lyons A. J. Newsome Sir Stanley Harley	The Earl of Aylesford Dr. R. S. Rudland MBE R. P. R. Iliffe W. B. Harley
1974/1975	The 11th Earl of Aylesford	The Lord Iliffe The Lord Leigh P. H. V. Twist P. S. Rendall	Sir William Lyons A. J. Newsome Sir Stanley Harley The Hon. Henry Feilding	Dr. R. S. Rudland MBE R. P. R. Iliffe W. B. Harley The Earl of Aylesford
1975/1976	Robert Peter Richard Iliffe	No change		

Year				
1976/1977	William Burdess Harley		No change	Dr. R. S. Rudland MBE P. H. V. Twist P. S. Rendall The Earl of Aylesford
1977/1978	The Hon. Henry Feilding	The Lord Iliffe A. J. Newsome Sir Stanley Harley The Hon. Henry Feilding	Sir William Lyons R. P. R. Iliffe W. B. Harley	Dr. R. S. Rudland MBE P. H. V. Twist The Earl of Aylesford
1978/1979	The Lord Iliffe	The Lord Iliffe A. J. Newsome W. B. Harley	Sir William Lyons R. P. R. Iliffe The Hon. Henry Feilding Lord Guernsey	A. J. Newsome W. B. Harley The Earl of Aylesford
1979/80	Dr. Robert Spencer Rudland	The Lord Iliffe R. P. R. Iliffe Lord Guernsey	Dr. R. S. Rudland MBE P. H. V. Twist The Hon. Henry Feilding J. S. Feilding	A. J. Newsome W. H. Harley The Earl of Aylesford D. L. Burbidge
1980/1981	Patrick Haze Vivian Twist	The Lord Iliffe R. P. R. Iliffe Lord Guernsey J. E. Feilding	Dr. R. S. Rudland MBE P. H. V. Twist The Hon. Henry Feilding I. W. Liggins	A. J. Newsome W. H. Harley The Earl of Aylesford D. L. Burbidge
1981/1982	Alan J. Newsome		No change	
1982/1983	The 11th Earl of Aylesford		No change	
1983/1984	Dr. Robert Spencer Rudland		No change	
1984/1985	Robert Peter Richard Iliffe	The Lord Iliffe R. P. R. Iliffe The Hon. Henry Feilding I. W. Liggins	Dr. R. S. Rudland MBE P. H. V. Twist Lord Guernsey	A. J. Newsome The Earl of Aylesford D. L. Burbidge J. S. Feilding
1985/1986	The Hon. Henry Feilding		No change	
1986/1987	Lord Guernsey	The Lord Iliffe R. P. R. Iliffe J. S. Feilding R. H. P. Spencer	Dr. R. S. Rudland MBE The Hon. Henry Feilding I. W. Liggins	A. J. Newsome Lord Guernsey D. C. Burbidge The Earl of Aylesford
1987/1988	J. S. Feilding		No change	

Appendix III

Acknowledgements and a modest reading list

In general, I have noted the source of quotations by a brief mention in the text, so that by referring to the list of books which follows, readers will I hope be able to pursue any aspect in more detail. I am grateful to the authors mentioned, and to their publishers, for being able to make these quotations.

The book could not have appeared in this form without the help of Mr Roger Vaughan of the Coventry Archives, where Cappers' records have been kept for some years. Later, when Mr Vaughan became City Heritage Officer, Coventry Museums and Galleries, he and Mr Martin Roberts, Keeper of Social History, kindly gave permission for current members of the Cappers' Company to use material from an exhibition at the Herbert Art Gallery and Museum in Coventry to illustrate this book.

Mr Vaughan also introduced me to Mr Anthony Divett, who transcribed much of the material in the Accounts and Orders Books which, as noted above, the Cappers had deposited in the Coventry Archives, and Mr Divett also helped generally with comment and advice on the direction of the book.

The point should be made, however, that the opinions expressed are my own, except those that are, directly or indirectly, the quotations of others, and any errors my responsibility.

Amongst the library staff who have given me valuable assistance are those at the Coventry Archives, at Coventry Central Library, at the Bodleian Library, University of Oxford, at Stockport Central Library, and at the Hat Museum in that town. Other library staff who helped me included those at the Guildhall, London, at the Oxford City Central Library and at the library of Warwick University.

The Cappers themselves have of course been generous with information, and I should mention also the former Managing Directors of Cash's nametape concern, Mr James Graham.

As for the Reading list, I give this by grouping the books under a heading referring to the most appropriate chapter.

AUTHOR'S NOTE

Miss Mary Dormer Harris's book was, I believe, privately printed for the Cappers in 1921, though an imprint states that it was published by Cornwall Press. Few copies exist today.

INTRODUCTION

P.M. Giles, 'The felt-hatting industry c. 1500-1850 with particular reference to Lancashire and Cheshire', *Transactions of the Lancashire & Cheshire antiquarian Society, Vol LXIX (1959), 104-132.*

J. H. Smith, 'The development of the English felt and silk hat trade 1500-1912'. Unpublished Ph.D. thesis, University of Manchester, Department of History.

CHAPTER 1

There are many books on medieval England; I make no claim to have chosen the best. Those named have, however, been particularly useful.

Joan Evans (ed.). *The Flowering Middle Ages*,
Thames & Hudson (1966).

Friedrich Heer, *The Medieval Word, Europe 1100-1350*,
Weidenfeld & Nicolson (1961).

R.W. Southern, *The Making of the Middle Ages*,
Hutchinson (1968).

Carlo M. Cipoll, *Before the Industrial Revolution 1000-1700*,
Methuen (1976).

J.L. Bolton, *The Medieval English Economy 1150-1500*, Dent (1985).

CHAPTER II

Eileen Power, *Medieval Women*, Cambridge University Press (1975).

J. Huizinga, *The Waning of the Middle Ages* (Lieden, 1924).

CHAPTER III

William Herbert, *The History of the Twelve Great Livery Companies of London*, two vols, (1834). Reprinted by David & Charles (Publishers) Ltd.

E. Lipson, *A Short History of Wool and its Manufacture*, William Heinemann (1953).

'*Coventry through the Ages*', compiled by D.H. Smith, Coventry Branch of the Historical Association, Pamphlet No. 19 (1992).

Mary Hulton, '*True as Coventry Blue*', Coventry Branch of the Historical Association, Pamphlet No. 21 (1997).

Charles V. Pythian-Adam, *Desolation of a City*, Cambridge University Press (1979).

Mary Dormer Harris (ed.), *Coventry Leet Book 1420-1555*, (London, 1907-13).

The Victoria Histories of the Counties of England, Warwick (London, 1947).

CHAPTER IV

Pamela King, *Coventry Mystery Plays*, The Coventry Branch of the Historical Association, Pamphlet No. 22 (1997).

Reginald Ingram, *Records of Early English Drama: Coventry* (Toronto, 1981).

Hardin Craig, '*Two Coventry Corpus Christi Plays*', Early English Text Society (London, 1957).

Rosemary Woolf, *The English Mystery Plays* (London, 1972).

Alice Lynes, *Coventry's Miracle Plays*, Coventry City Libraries Local History, Pamphlet No. 1 (1963).

Benjamin Poole, *History of Coventry: Its History and Antiquities*, John Russell Smith (London, 1870).

Thomas Sharp, *Antiquities of Coventry*, Hall and English (London, 1871).

CHAPTER V

Ronald M. Berger, *The Most Necessary Luxuries – The Mercers' Company of Coventry 1550-80*, Pennsylvania State University Press (1993).

W. H. B. Court, *The Rise of the Midland Industries 1600-1838*, Oxford University Press (1965).

CHAPTER VI

John Prest, *The Industrial Revolution in Coventry*, Oxford University Press (1960).

George Eliot, *Middlemarch, A Study of Provincial Life* (London, 1871-2).

CHAPTER VII

Kenneth Richardson, *20th-Century Coventry*, Macmillan (1972).

Peter King, *The Motor Men*, Quiller Press (1989).

Jonathan Wood, *Wheels of Misfortune*, Sidgwick & Jackson (1988).

INDEX

Indexer's note: Names of individual Cappers mentioned in the text appear in the index but for a list of Masters and Members 1900–2000 readers should refer to pp153- 62. Page numbers in italic refer to captions to illustrations.

Opposite: The table in the Cappers
Room set with simple bread and
wine for their meeting in the year
2000. On the wall is the modern
tapestry they commissioned to
replace that lost in the Blitz.